4

# Wonderful WORLD

**SECOND EDITION**

**STUDENT'S BOOK**

NATIONAL GEOGRAPHIC
LEARNING

Australia • Brazil • Japan • Korea • Mexico • Singapore • Spain • United Kingdom • United States

# Contents

# Numbers to 100,000

**1,000** *one thousand*
**10,000** *ten thousand*
**15,000** *fifteen thousand*
**50,000** *fifty thousand*
**100,000** *one hundred thousand*

**6,791** → *six thousand, seven hundred and ninety-one*
**42,975** → *forty-two thousand, nine hundred and seventy-five*
**98,153** → *ninety-eight thousand, one hundred and fifty-three*

**1 Listen. Circle the number.** TR: 0.2

1 15,000 1,500 1,050
2 7,615 76,015 67,015
3 1,984 12,894 12,984
4 63,948 63,498 69,348
5 97,80 19,781 97,081

**2 Read and write the digits.**

1 two thousand, eight hundred and forty-six

______________________

2 seventeen thousand, nine hundred and three

______________________

3 fifty-four thousand, seven hundred and fourteen

______________________

4 seventy-nine thousand and eight

______________________

5 thirty-two thousand, five hundred and ninety six

______________________

# Years and dates

Today is **Wednesday, 12 July 2020**.
The war took place **in the year 1486**.
That was the **fifteenth century**.
The family lived in that house for two **decades**, from 1999 to 2019.

**1 Circle the correct words.**

1 Tomorrow is **the twenty first-century / Thursday, 7 October.**
2 A **decade / century** is ten years.
3 A **decade / century** is one hundred years.
4 She was born on **the fifteenth century / Sunday, 30 June.**
5 The explorers first visited the island in the **eighteenth century / decade**.

**2 Write the century for each year.**

1 1892 ______________________
2 1940 ______________________
3 2018 ______________________
4 1250 ______________________

# Subject and object pronouns

**Subject pronouns:** I, you, he, she, it, we, you, they
**Object pronouns:** me, you, him, her, it, us, you, them

**1 Complete the table.**

| Subject pronouns | Object pronouns |
|---|---|
| I | |
| you | |
| | him |
| she | |
| | it |
| we | |
| you | |
| | them |

# Possessive adjectives

**Possessive adjectives:**
my, your, his, her, its, our, your, their

**1 Circle the correct words.**

1 My dad is 35 years old. **His / Her** birthday is in April.

2 I'm Sofia and this is **her / my** sister, Ava.

3 We want to go to the cinema to watch **their / our** favourite film.

4 Look at that cat. **Your / Its** eyes are blue!

5 Ben and Tony are brothers and **their / our** mother is my teacher.

# There is/are/was/were

**There is** one book on the table.
**There aren't** any pens.

**There were** three biscuits in my lunch box.
**There wasn't** a drink.

**1 Complete the sentences with is, are, was or were.**

1 There ________ three students in the room yesterday.

2 ________ there any oranges in the kitchen now?

3 ________ there a pencil on the desk a few minutes ago?

4 There ________ lots of good books in this library. Which do you want?

5 There ________ a pizza in the kitchen. We can share it.

# Question words

**Question words:** how, what, where, when, who, whose

**When** are we meeting? **Whose** jacket is this?

**1 Complete the questions.**

1 '________ is that boy?' 'That's Lee.'

2 '________ bag is that? Is it Sarita's?'

3 '________ did Jim say about his present?'

4 '________ do you live?' 'At 46 Baker Street.'

5 '________ did you visit us?' 'Last summer.'

6 '________ do we get to the train station?' 'Turn left here, and it's on the right.'

# Prepositions of place

**Remember!**

**1 Circle the correct words.**

1  The red door is **between / behind** two white doors.

2  The frog is **under / in** the leaf.

3  The girl is **behind / in front of** the red curtain.

4  The dog is **on / next to** the boy.

**2 Talk about where your things are with a partner. Use prepositions of place and words like *book, pencil, school bag,* etc.**

# 1 Being Together

Honey bees around the queen cell containing larvae

**1 Why are the honey bees working together?**

- [ ] to grow flowers
- [ ] to sting people
- [ ] to protect their leader

# Lesson 1

a great time
Look at the time!
on time
time for
waste (one's) time

**1** Listen. Listen and repeat. TR: 1.1

**2** Listen and read. TR: 1.2

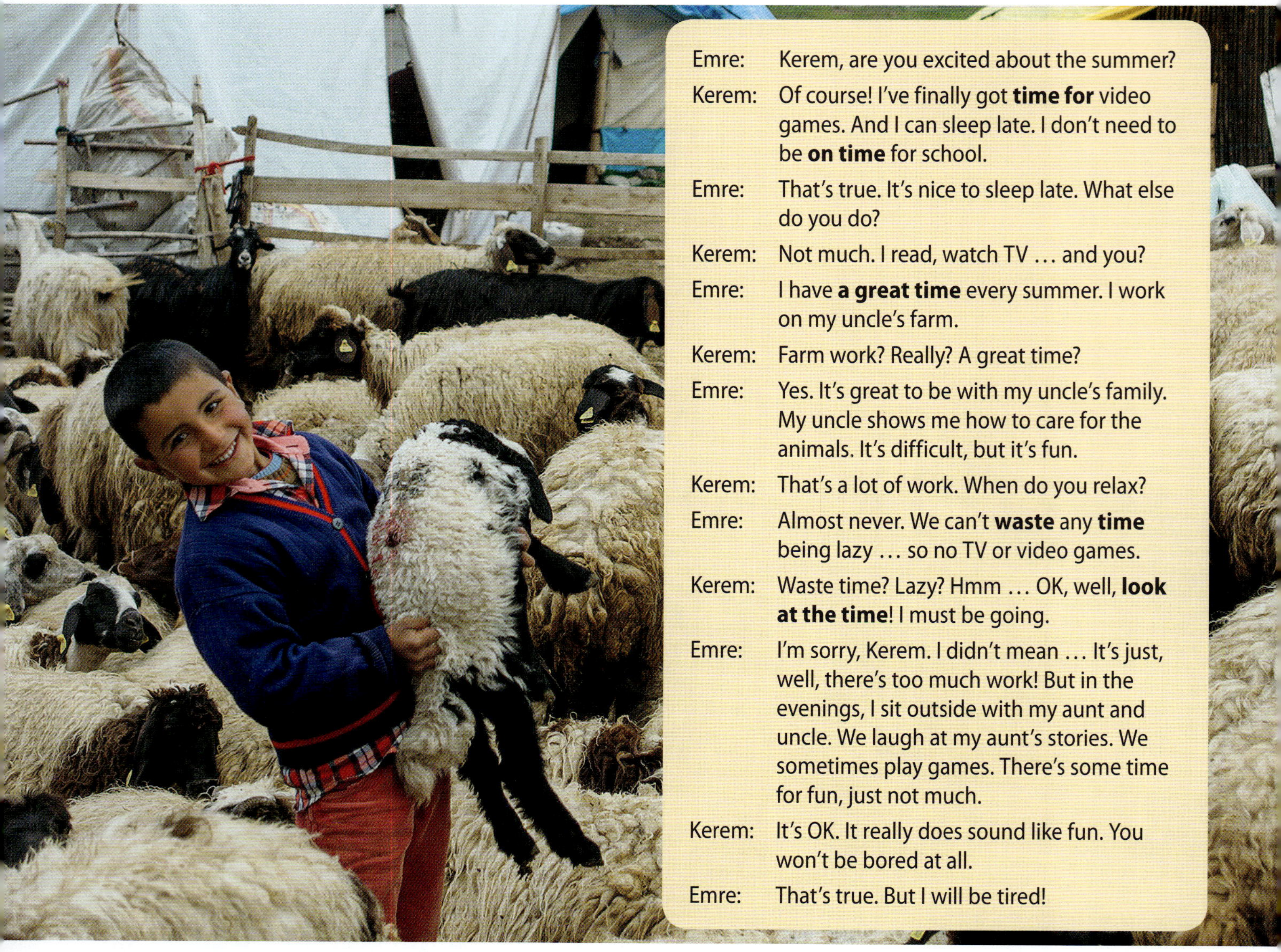

Emre: Kerem, are you excited about the summer?

Kerem: Of course! I've finally got **time for** video games. And I can sleep late. I don't need to be **on time** for school.

Emre: That's true. It's nice to sleep late. What else do you do?

Kerem: Not much. I read, watch TV … and you?

Emre: I have **a great time** every summer. I work on my uncle's farm.

Kerem: Farm work? Really? A great time?

Emre: Yes. It's great to be with my uncle's family. My uncle shows me how to care for the animals. It's difficult, but it's fun.

Kerem: That's a lot of work. When do you relax?

Emre: Almost never. We can't **waste** any **time** being lazy … so no TV or video games.

Kerem: Waste time? Lazy? Hmm … OK, well, **look at the time**! I must be going.

Emre: I'm sorry, Kerem. I didn't mean … It's just, well, there's too much work! But in the evenings, I sit outside with my aunt and uncle. We laugh at my aunt's stories. We sometimes play games. There's some time for fun, just not much.

Kerem: It's OK. It really does sound like fun. You won't be bored at all.

Emre: That's true. But I will be tired!

**3** **Complete the sentences with the phrases from Activity 1.**

1 Here's Mum – she's always ________________.

2 Hurry up! We haven't got ________________ a chat.

3 Don't ________________! Get back to work!

4 Have ________________ on holiday, Grandad!

5 Oh, ________________! I'm late again.

**4** **Circle the correct words.**

1 During the school year, Kerem **has** / **hasn't** got much time for video games.

2 In the summer, Emre has a great time **playing video games** / **working on a farm**.

3 Emre can't **waste time** / **be on time** when he's at his uncle's farm.

4 On his uncle's farm, Emre relaxes by **watching TV** / **sitting outside** with his family.

5 At the end of the summer, Emre will be **bored** / **tired**.

## 5 Listen. Listen and repeat. TR: 1.3

| | |
|---|---|
| **enjoy** | I enjoy working on our farm. |
| **grandchild** | Gilda spends time with her grandchild while his parents work. |
| **laugh** | We're laughing because this film is very funny. |
| **lazy** | The lazy cat sleeps all day. |
| **only child** | Serena hasn't got brothers or sisters. She's an only child. |
| **nephew** | Gil is Uncle Ed's favourite nephew. |
| **niece** | My niece is my sister's daughter. |

## 6 Complete the sentences with words from Activity 5.

1 I'm the youngest of my grandparents' three ________________.

2 Tony is an ________________. He hasn't got any brothers or sisters.

3 I'm one of Aunt Ana's seven ________________. We're all boys!

4 Do you ________________ riding horses?

5 This film makes me ________________. The actors are very funny.

6 Please get up! It's eleven o'clock. Don't be ________________.

### GRAMMAR Present simple

We use the present simple to talk about:

**a** general truths.
*It **rains** a lot in winter here.*

**b** things we do regularly.
*I **visit** my uncle every summer.*

**c** permanent states.
*Uncle Omar **lives** on a farm.*

## 7 Complete the sentences with the present simple of the words in brackets.

1 ________________ you ________________ TV with your sisters? (watch)

2 We ________________ at the weekends. We stay at home. (not work)

3 Emre ________________ the farm is fun. (think)

4 My uncle ________________ breakfast. (not eat)

### GRAMMAR Adverbs of frequency

We use these adverbs to show how often we do something.

*My friends **sometimes** come to my house.*

**always → usually → often → sometimes → never**

100% of the time ←——→ 0% of the time

Adverbs of frequency go before the main verb:

*They **never see** Grandad.*

**But** they go **after** the verb **be**:

*My friend **is never** on time.*

Except in a question:

***Is** your mum **always** so nice?*

You can ask questions with **How often**.

***How often** do you go on holiday?*

## 8 Put the words in the correct order.

1 see / always / school / I / cousin / after / my

________________________________

2 ? / for / on time / Mum / is / usually / work

________________________________

3 am / I / never / school / for / late

________________________________

4 ? / how / visit / do / often / you / Grandma

________________________________

## 9 Listen to Sally say what she does with her family. Circle the correct answers. TR: 1.4

1 Sally visits her grandparents **twice** / **once** a week.

2 Sally **always** / **sometimes** has banana ice cream on Saturdays.

3 Dad **never** / **often** goes on holiday to the sea.

4 Tilly goes to the park every **Monday** / **Saturday**.

## 10 How often do you and your family do these things? Tell your partner. Use adverbs of frequency.

| | |
|---|---|
| cook | go on holiday |
| visit grandparents | watch TV |

## 11 Write five sentences about how often you do things. Use a different adverb of frequency in each one.

# Lesson 2

**1** **Listen. Listen and repeat.** TR: 1.5

hunt

hurt

protect

danger
kill
population

**2** **Listen and read.** TR: 1.6

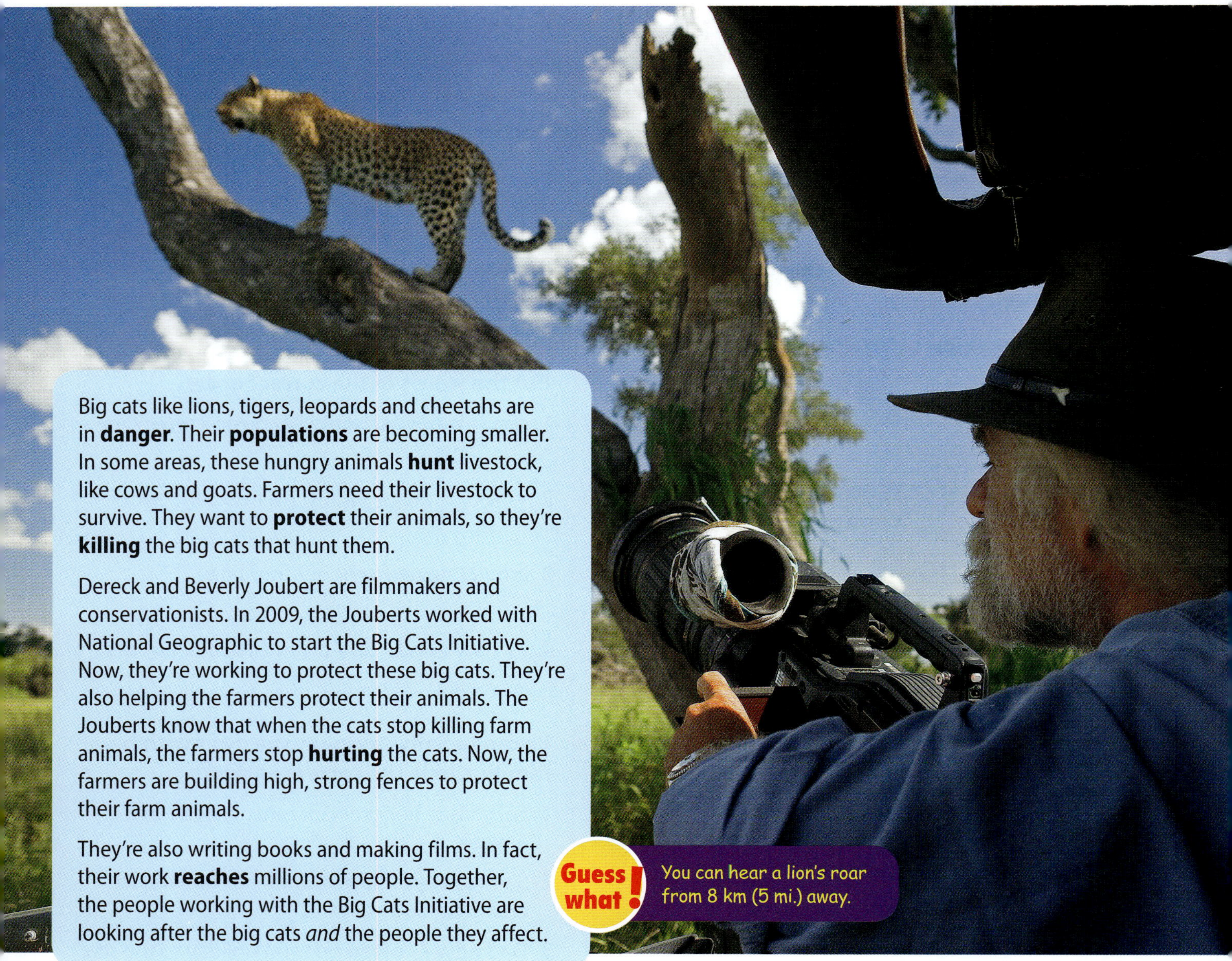

Big cats like lions, tigers, leopards and cheetahs are in **danger**. Their **populations** are becoming smaller. In some areas, these hungry animals **hunt** livestock, like cows and goats. Farmers need their livestock to survive. They want to **protect** their animals, so they're **killing** the big cats that hunt them.

Dereck and Beverly Joubert are filmmakers and conservationists. In 2009, the Jouberts worked with National Geographic to start the Big Cats Initiative. Now, they're working to protect these big cats. They're also helping the farmers protect their animals. The Jouberts know that when the cats stop killing farm animals, the farmers stop **hurting** the cats. Now, the farmers are building high, strong fences to protect their farm animals.

They're also writing books and making films. In fact, their work **reaches** millions of people. Together, the people working with the Big Cats Initiative are looking after the big cats *and* the people they affect.

**Guess what!** You can hear a lion's roar from 8 km (5 mi.) away.

**3** **Read. Tick T for *True* or F for *False*.**

1 Livestock is hunting big cats, so their population is going down. T F

2 Farmers are killing big cats to protect their farm animals. T F

3 The Jouberts help the farmers protect their animals. T F

4 The Jouberts work to tell others about the danger big cats are in. T F

5 Millions of people are affected by big cats. T F

**4** **Circle the correct word.**

1 The **danger** / **population** of our town is 25,000 people.

2 Hungry lions **protect** / **kill** farm animals for food.

3 Leopards are a species in **danger** / **population**.

4 Leopards like to **hunt** / **hurt** at night.

5 People need to work together to **protect** / **hunt** big cats.

## 5 Listen. Listen and repeat. TR: 1.7

| | |
|---|---|
| **care for** | A vet cares for sick animals. |
| **frightened of** | Many people are frightened of lions. |
| **in fact** | My camera doesn't work. In fact, I'm buying a new one today. |
| **look after** | Farmers must look after their animals. |
| **reach** | Smartphones can help information to quickly reach many people. |

## 6 Circle the correct words.

1 We can **reach** / **look after** Mum on her phone.

2 There's no school tomorrow. **In fact** / **Let's reach**, we're on holiday for two weeks.

3 We must **look after** / **be frightened of** big cats to help them survive.

4 My aunt **cares for** / **reaches** six children, including three nieces and nephews.

5 The baby is **frightened of** / **in fact** the leopard at the zoo.

### GRAMMAR Present continuous

We use the present continuous to talk about:

**a** things that are temporary or are happening now or around now.
*Uncle Dan* ***is eating*** *breakfast.*
*He****'s not having*** *tea with his breakfast.*

**b** fixed future plans.
*I****'m visiting*** *my friend tomorrow.*
***Are*** *you* ***coming*** *with us?*

**c** what is happening in a picture.
*In this picture, the lion cub* ***is playing****.*
***Is*** *its mother* ***sleeping*** *in the picture?*
*No, she* ***isn't****.*

**Time expressions** now, at the moment, today, this morning, tomorrow

## 7 Use the picture below to complete the sentences with the present continuous form of the verbs in the box.

| eat | play | run | sit | sleep |
|---|---|---|---|---|

1 There's a monkey. It ________________ in the tree.

2 The giraffe ________________ leaves.

3 Look! The zebras are frightened. They ________________ away.

4 The mother lion is tired. In fact, she ________________ .

5 There are two lion cubs. They ________________ .

## 8 Listen to Laura and Helen and tick T for *True* or F for *False*. TR: 1.8

1 Laura is going shopping. T F

2 Laura is meeting Lisa at three o'clock. T F

3 Laura is going to the cinema. T F

4 Laura's grandma is eating dinner at home. T F

5 Helen is going out for dinner. T F

### SOUNDS OF ENGLISH TR: 1.9

Listen and circle the sentence you hear.

1 a I'm eating Lisa in the park.
b I'm meeting Lisa in the park.

2 a We're working tomorrow.
b We're walking tomorrow.

3 a Are you talking, Jane?
b Are you taking Jane?

# Lesson 3

**1 Listen and read about Marta's family. Write the correct name under each picture.** TR: 1.10

## My Family

Hello! I'm Marta Romero and this is my family! We live on a farm. It's really cool.

I'm ten years old and I go to Minerva Secondary School. I play the piano. I have lessons every Saturday. It's great! Next week I'm playing the piano at a party. In this picture I'm not playing music. I'm sitting on the grass.

There's a picture of my brother, Samuel, too. He's twelve and he likes football. He's OK, but he's very lazy sometimes! At the moment, he's staying with our cousin in Colombia. He's coming back next month.

The photo of the diver is of Mum on holiday last year. She really loves swimming and diving. My dad doesn't swim. He likes watching football on TV instead. In the picture, he's watching a World Cup match.

The other picture is of my horse, Ollie. He eats grass and carrots. In the photo, he's running. He's really fast!

**2 Change the words in bold to make the sentences true.**

1 Marta has piano lessons every **day**. ____________

2 Marta is playing the piano at **school** next week. ____________

3 Samuel is staying with his **grandparents**. ____________

4 Dad likes **swimming**. ____________

5 Ollie is a **boy**. ____________

6 Ollie is good at **football**. ____________

### SAY IT LIKE THIS!

**Emphasising with *so***

It's so frightening!
She's so lazy!

**Complete the dialogues with these phrases. Then practise saying them with your partner.**

**Mum:** Diana never helps at home!
**Dad:** ____________

**Boy:** Look at that lion!
**Girl:** Ahh! ____________

## GRAMMAR Present simple and present continuous

We use the present simple to talk about general truths, things we do regularly and permanent states.
*We **live** in a big house.*

We use the present continuous to talk about things that are temporary or are happening now or around now, for fixed future plans and to say what is happening in a picture.
***I'm going out** with my cousin tomorrow.*

**Note:** There are some verbs that we don't use with continuous tenses. These are called **stative verbs** and they include *know, like, love, think, understand* and *want*.

**3 Complete the sentences using the present simple or the present continuous of the verbs in brackets.**

1 Look, the lion ________________ (roar)!
2 Grandad and Grandma ________________ (go) to the zoo this afternoon.
3 My friends and I ________________ (play) football every Saturday.
4 I never ________________ (visit) my cousins.
5 We ________________ (go) to horse riding lessons every week.
6 Oh, no! The animals ________________ (fight) again!

**4 Complete the sentences with these words. Use the present simple or the present continuous.**

come love not understand want write

1 I ______________ my cat very much.
2 ______________ your sister ______________ an ice cream?
3 ______________ Mum ______________ an email to Grandma now?
4 ______________ Uncle John ______________ to the park?
5 I ______________ this word. What does it mean?

## WRITING Time expressions and adverbs of frequency

**A Write PS next to the words we use with the present simple and PC next to the words we use with the present continuous.**

| | | | |
|---|---|---|---|
| at the moment | ____ | now | ____ |
| every day | ____ | once a week | ____ |
| this winter | ____ | sometimes | ____ |
| never | ____ | today | ____ |
| next month | ____ | always | ____ |

**B Read the description. Circle the correct time expressions or adverbs of frequency.**

Hello,
I'm Tai and this is my family! I am twelve years old and I go to Shogakko School. I have swimming lessons (1) **twice a week** / **now**. I go on holiday (2) **this summer** / **every summer** and I (3) **always** / **today** swim in the sea. My twin brother Jiro is between my parents. (4) **At the moment** / **Sometimes**, he's visiting our grandparents in Tokyo but he's coming back on Sunday night. Mum and Dad are laughing in the picture. They are (5) **always** / **this morning** happy!

**C Write a description of your family. Use this plan to help you.**

**Paragraph 1** All about me
**Paragraph 2** My brothers and sisters (or aunt/uncle/cousin etc)
**Paragraph 3** My parents
**Paragraph 4** My best friend (or My pet)

**D Remember to use time expressions and adverbs of frequency in your description.**

# 2 Where Do You Live?

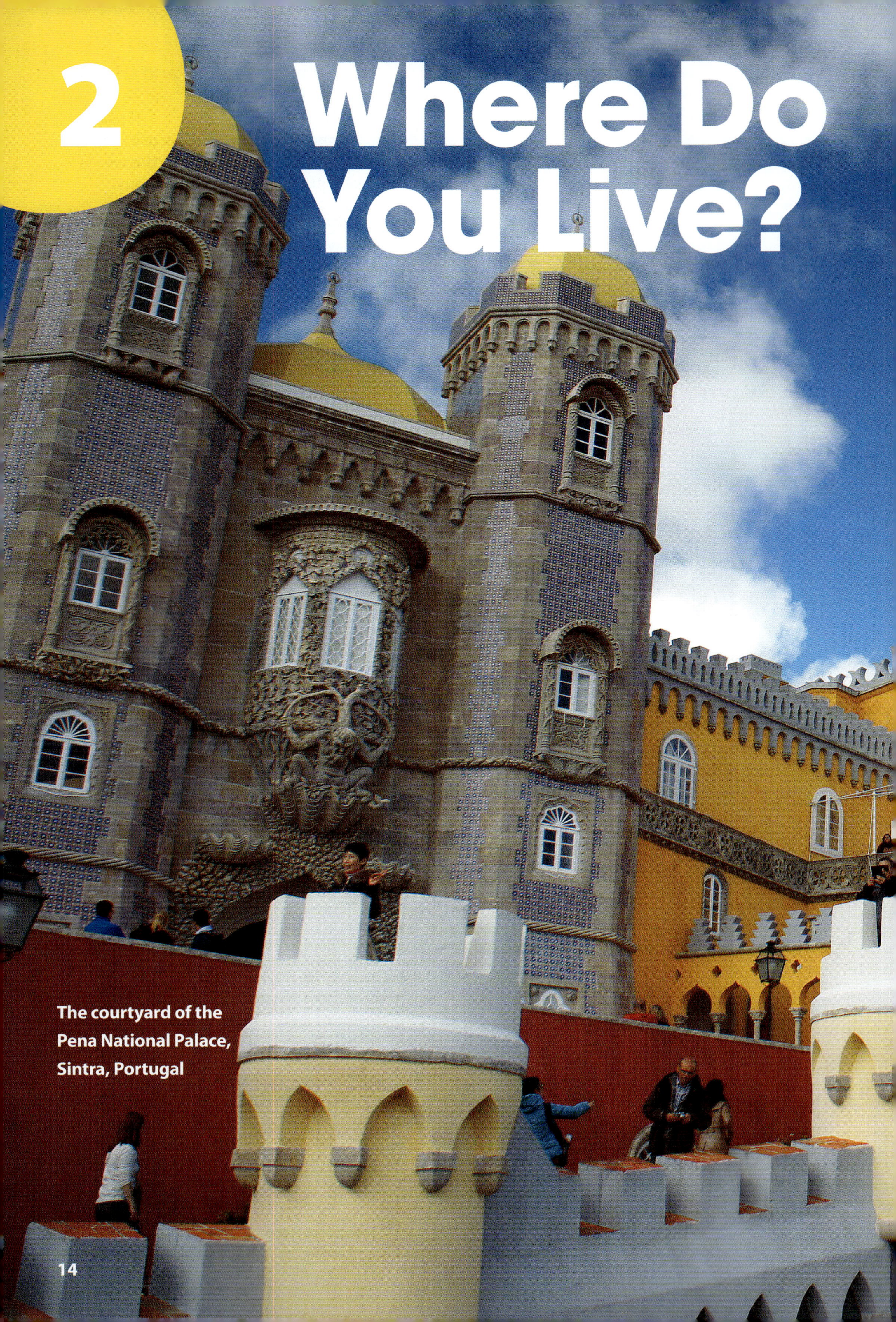

The courtyard of the Pena National Palace, Sintra, Portugal

1 **Tick the things you can see in the picture.**

- [ ] a door
- [ ] windows
- [ ] a kitchen
- [ ] a garden
- [ ] a clock

# Lesson 1

**1** **Listen. Listen and repeat.** TR: 2.1

pay

save (money)

awful
careful
hate
rich

**2** **Listen and read.** TR: 2.2

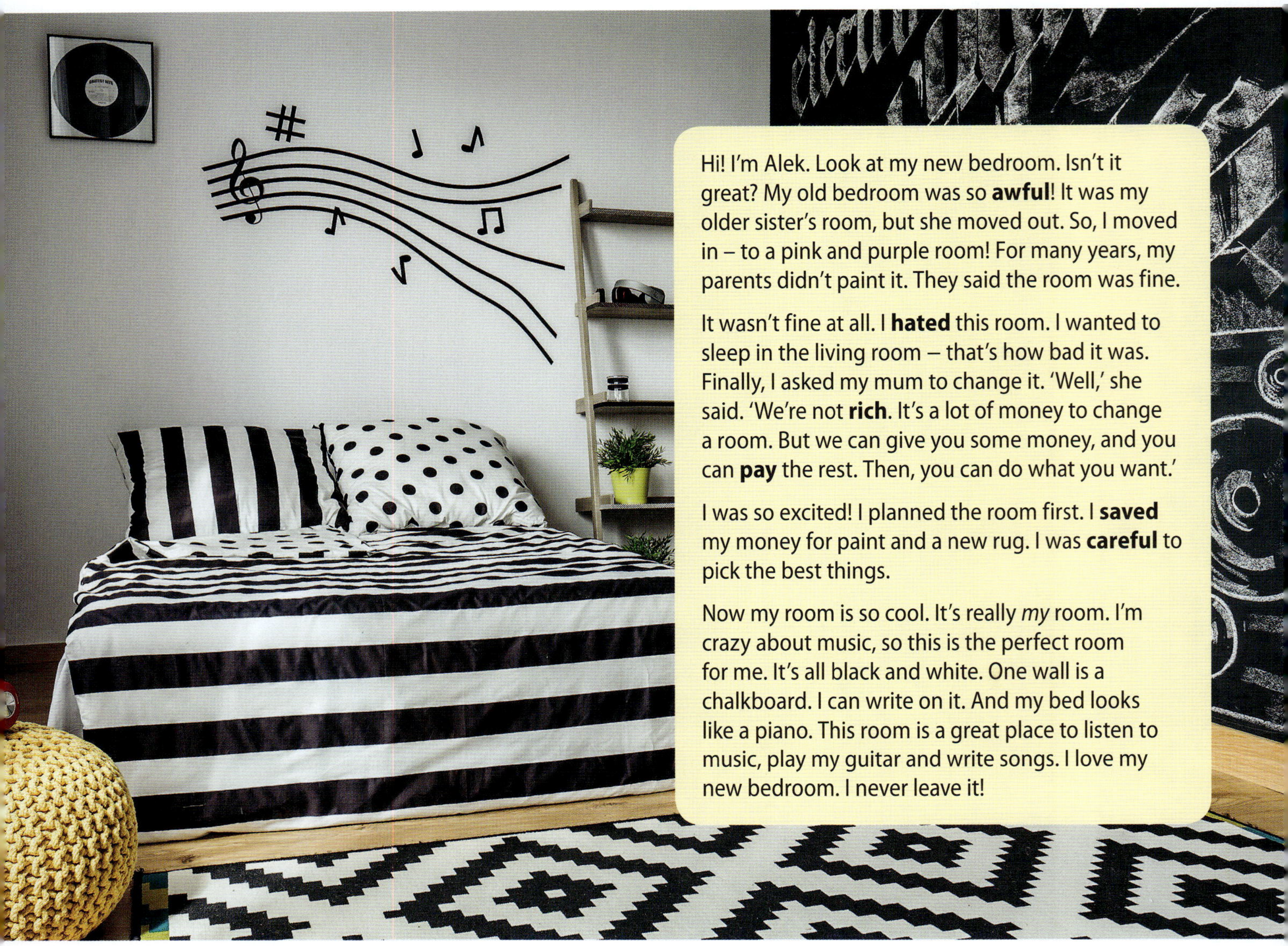

Hi! I'm Alek. Look at my new bedroom. Isn't it great? My old bedroom was so **awful**! It was my older sister's room, but she moved out. So, I moved in – to a pink and purple room! For many years, my parents didn't paint it. They said the room was fine.

It wasn't fine at all. I **hated** this room. I wanted to sleep in the living room – that's how bad it was. Finally, I asked my mum to change it. 'Well,' she said. 'We're not **rich**. It's a lot of money to change a room. But we can give you some money, and you can **pay** the rest. Then, you can do what you want.'

I was so excited! I planned the room first. I **saved** my money for paint and a new rug. I was **careful** to pick the best things.

Now my room is so cool. It's really *my* room. I'm crazy about music, so this is the perfect room for me. It's all black and white. One wall is a chalkboard. I can write on it. And my bed looks like a piano. This room is a great place to listen to music, play my guitar and write songs. I love my new bedroom. I never leave it!

**3** **Write the correct word.**

1 To give money to someone

__ __ __

2 To really dislike something

__ __ __ __

3 To keep money in a bank

__ __ __ __

4 Very, very bad

__ __ __ __ __

5 Having a lot of money

__ __ __ __

**4** **Read and match.**

| | | | |
|---|---|---|---|
| 1 | Alek's sister's old bedroom | a | leaves his new room. |
| 2 | When he had his old room, Alek | b | said the old room was fine. |
| 3 | Alek's parents | c | was pink. |
| 4 | Alek was careful | d | is perfect for him. |
| 5 | Alek's new room | e | hated it. |
| 6 | Alek never | f | to pick the best things. |

## GRAMMAR Past simple (regular verbs)

We use the past simple for:

**a** things that started and finished in the past.
*We **moved** here last year.*
*__Did__ you __live__ nearby?*
*No, we **didn't**.*

**b** things that happened one after the other in the past.
*We **cleaned** the house, **opened** the door and **walked** down the street.*

**c** habits in the past.
*I **tidied** my bedroom every Friday night.*

**Time expressions**

yesterday
last night/week/month/year
two days/a month/a year ago
in October/2007

**5** **Re-read the paragraph on page 16. Underline the verbs that end in *-ed*. How many are there?**

**6** **Complete the sentences with the past simple of the verbs in brackets.**

1 Ming ____________ (not want) a new bed.

2 The children ____________ (arrive) at Grandma's house an hour ago.

3 Leo ____________ (move) to the city in February.

4 I ____________ (not tidy) the kitchen.

5 ____________ (Oliver/visit) the new flat?

6 Why ____________ (they/stay) at home?

**7** **Listen. Listen and repeat.** TR: 2.3

armchair

coffee table

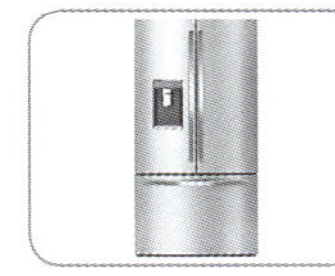
fridge

oven

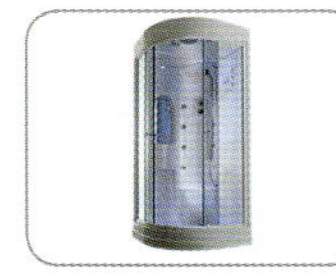
shower

sink

sofa

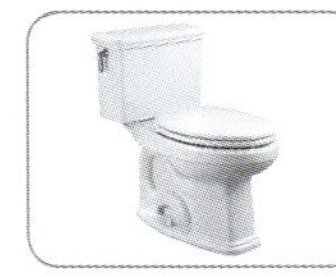
toilet

wardrobe

**8** **Match.**

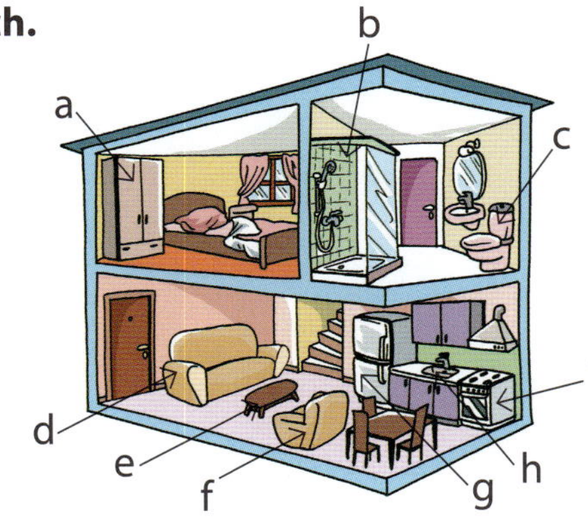


1 armchair ☐
2 coffee table ☐
3 fridge ☐
4 oven ☐
5 shower ☐
6 sink ☐
7 sofa ☐
8 toilet ☐
9 wardrobe ☐

**9** **Listen and number the pictures in the correct order.** TR: 2.4

☐ 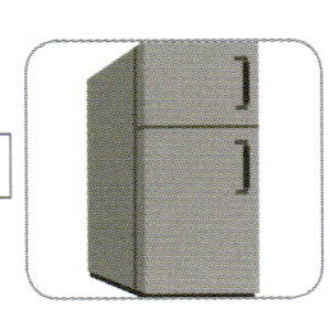 ☐ 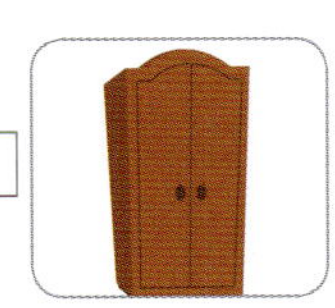 ☐ 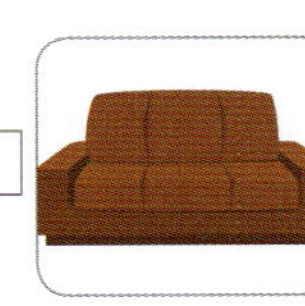

☐  ☐ 

**10** **Take it in turns to talk with a partner about when you did these things. Make notes.**

| tidy/my bedroom | arrive/at school |
|---|---|
| play/a sport or video game | visit/a friend |

**11** **Write four sentences about what your partner said in Activity 10. Use your notes.**

# Lesson 2

**1 Listen. Listen and repeat.** TR: 2.5

earthquake furniture glass modern plastic reuse rubbish

**2 Listen and read.** TR: 2.6

You just drank a bottle of water. Now, what do you do with the bottle? Do you put it in the **rubbish**? Recycle it? Or do you use it for something else? Bottled drinks create a lot of rubbish. But some people are **reusing** bottles in a very interesting way – by creating houses out of them.

In Puerto Iguazú, Argentina, artist Alfredo Santa Cruz and his family built the Ecological Bottle House. They made this house with many types of rubbish, but mostly **plastic** bottles. Even the **furniture** is made from old plastic bottles. In another Argentinian town, Quilmes, artist Rubén 'Tito' Ingenieri made his house from **glass** bottles. He worked on it for over 20 years. The inside has got a **modern** kitchen and bathroom. There's also a tall tower. All in all, the house is made from more than six million glass bottles! These artists want to teach visitors about how much people throw away. They also want people to use less and make less rubbish.

Maria Ponce lost her home in 2001, when a strong **earthquake** hit in El Salvador. Maria decided to build a new house in her village. She finished her house in 2005, when she was 76 years old. You can see it in this photo. It's very strong: the walls and roof are plastic bottles, and the floor is made from bottle tops. Maria is happy there because she enjoys the visitors who come to see her unusual home.

**Guess what!** In the village of Granados, Guatemala, there's a two-room school made from over 6,000 plastic bottles.

**3 Answer the questions.**

1 What are three things you can do with an old water bottle?
2 What's the Ecological Bottle House made of?
3 How many glass bottles did Ingenieri use to make his house?
4 What do the artists from Argentina want to teach people?
5 Why did Maria Ponce build her house from bottles?

**4 Complete the sentences with words from Activity 1.**

1 Please recycle the ______________ bottles.
2 The pictures came off the walls during the ______________.
3 A ______________ TV has got a computer in it.
4 Put the paper in the blue bin and the ______________ in the black bin.
5 How can we ______________ glass bottles?

## 5 Listen. Listen and repeat. TR: 2.7

balcony

bookcase

floor

microwave oven

roof

rug

vacuum cleaner

washing machine

## 6 Match.

1 balcony
2 bookcase
3 floor
4 microwave oven
5 roof
6 rug
7 vacuum cleaner
8 washing machine

a It's the top of a house.
b It cleans your clothes.
c You always stand on it.
d It cooks food fast.
e You put books on it.
f It cleans the floor.
g It's outside a flat.
h It covers the floor.

### GRAMMAR Past simple (irregular verbs)

We do not add **-ed** for the past simple affirmative of irregular verbs.

*Mum **gave** my aunt a vacuum cleaner.*

*We **got** a new bookcase yesterday.*

## 7 Complete the paragraph with the past simple of the verbs in brackets.

Last year we (1) ________ (sell) our house in the mountains. We (2) ________ (buy) a cottage by the sea. One day, I (3) ________ (find) a cat on the street. She didn't have a home and she (4) ________ (be) very sick. Every day she (5) ________ (come) to our new house and I (6) ________ (give) her food and water. Now she's my pet and my best friend!

## 8 Listen to the conversation and complete the sentences. TR: 2.8

1 Myles made some cool new ________.
2 He used old ________ bottles.
3 Lara asked if Myles made these things from ________.
4 Myles made four ________ and two ________.
5 Myles ________ his furniture, but he ________ photos of it first.
6 Myles got ________ euros in total for his furniture.

### SOUNDS OF ENGLISH TR: 2.9, 2.10

A Read these words aloud, paying attention to the sounds of the highlighted letters. What are the two different sounds?

| | |
|---|---|
| 1 yell**ow** | 5 h**ow** |
| 2 sh**ow**er | 6 sn**ow** |
| 3 n**ow** | 7 br**ow**n |
| 4 kn**ow** | 8 sh**ow** |

B Now put the words in A in the correct columns. Listen and check your answers.

| bel**ow** | t**ow**n |
|---|---|
| ________ | ________ |
| ________ | ________ |
| ________ | ________ |
| ________ | ________ |

## 9 Work in pairs. Choose an item from Activity 5 and describe it. Don't name the item. Can your partner guess the item?

This is tall. It's got shelves. You have it in your living room.

Is it a bookcase?

## 10 Discuss the following in pairs.

1 What things do you reuse? What do you throw away?
2 What is something unusual that you made? What did you use to make it?
3 What can you do to create less rubbish? Name three things.

# Lesson 3

**1 Listen and read the descriptions. Write the correct names under the pictures.** TR: 2.11

## My Home

**Jian, 10**
My family and I live in a houseboat. It's small but it's got two bedrooms, a kitchen and a bathroom. There's a large table with chairs in the kitchen. There's also a microwave oven for cooking. It's even got a washing machine. It's really cool!

**Omar, 12**
We lived in a large flat next to a river for many years. We had a beautiful sitting room and a long balcony with a great view of a large garden. But it was too big. So last year we moved into a small, modern house. Now we live near my grandparents. We visit them often.

**Ingrid, 11**
My family and I live in a huge old house in the centre of town. It's got seven bedrooms, three bathrooms and two sitting rooms. I'm an only child, so we don't use all the rooms. Some rooms haven't got any furniture at all, and there isn't a very nice view from my bedroom. I don't hate my home, but I don't love it either!

**Katia, 14**
We bought our flat three years ago. We haven't got a garden but we've got a big balcony and a beautiful dining room with a view of a park. I really like our home.

**2 Write J (Jian), O (Omar), I (Ingrid) or K (Katia). Who …**

1 can see a park from his/her home? ☐
2 mentions appliances in his/her home? ☐
3 lives in a very big house? ☐
4 talks about a home he/she doesn't live in now? ☐
5 moved into his/her house three years ago? ☐

### SAY IT LIKE THIS!

**Talking about homes**
Where do you live?
I live in a town/a flat/a houseboat, etc.
I moved into my house six months/two years ago.
My house is big/small/old/modern.

**Complete and practise with your partner.**

(1) ________________ do you live?
(2) ________________ in a cottage in a village.
(3) ________________ the cottage two years ago.
Is your cottage old? No, (4) ________________.

**3** **Listen to the conversation. Change the words in bold to make the sentences true.** TR: 2.12

1 Paula visited her cousin's new **flat**. ______
2 It's really **nice**. ______
3 It's very **big**. ______
4 It's got **modern** furniture. ______
5 The garden is full of **flowers**. ______
6 Paula's cousin wanted to live in the **city**. ______

**4** **Talk about the flat in the picture with your partner.**

## WRITING Linking words

**A** **Read about these linking words.**

We use **and** to add something else to a sentence.
*This flat is old **and** small.*

We use **but** to show contrast (when two things are different).
*The sitting room is small **but** beautiful.*

We use **because** before the reason for something.
*I don't like my bedroom **because** it's very small.*

We use **so** before the result of something.
*I don't cook **so** I don't need an oven.*

**B** **Circle the correct words.**

1 My bed is big **and** / **but** it isn't comfortable.
2 This rug is horrible **because** / **so** I want a new one.
3 The stairs are old **and** / **but** dangerous.
4 I don't like this flat **because** / **so** the bedrooms are very small.

**C** **Read the advert and complete it with and, because, but and so.**

### House for sale

This fantastic house is in a beautiful village. It is great for large families (1) ______ it has got five bedrooms, three bathrooms (2) ______ a large sitting room. It has also got a very big kitchen with a great view of the pretty little garden. The house is modern (3) ______ some of the furniture is old. There are two schools in the same street, (4) ______ children can walk to school in two minutes. Come and see this great home soon!

**Call 234 5694 today!**

**D** **Write an advert for your home.**

**Answer these questions:**
What type of home do you live in (a house with a garden, a flat with a balcony, etc)?
Where is it?
Are there lots of rooms? What rooms are there?
Is it old or new?
Is the furniture modern?
What is near your house (schools, shops, etc)?

**E** **Read your advert and check that you have used and, but, because and so.**

# Review

## 1 Label the photos.

______

______

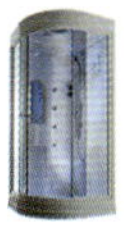
______

______

______

______

## 2 Match the opposites.

| | | | |
|---|---|---|---|
| 1 | hurt | a | late |
| 2 | reuse | b | old |
| 3 | on time | c | love |
| 4 | hate | d | protect |
| 5 | awful | e | throw away |
| 6 | modern | f | nice |

## 3 Complete the sentences with these words.

| | | |
|---|---|---|
| careful | frightened of | great time |
| population | time for | waste time |

1 Dad hasn't got ______ the match tonight. He's working late.

2 Are you ______ tigers? Or do you think they're cool?

3 The ______ of leopards is going down. We must protect them.

4 Ms Smith was ______ to count all her students before leaving the school.

5 There's lots to do. Let's not ______!

6 My friends went to the party and they had a ______.

## 4 Put the adverbs of frequency in brackets in the correct place.

1 We don't visit my aunt on Saturdays. (always)

______

2 They are at home in the morning. (never)

______

3 Are Ben and his sister on time for school? (usually)

______

4 My best friend comes to my house. (often)

______

5 Is your sitting room clean? (always)

______

6 Does your class reuse old paper? (sometimes)

______

## 5 Complete the sentences with the present simple or the present continuous of the verbs in brackets.

1 Look! The lion cub ______ (follow) its mother.

2 How often ______ (you meet) your friends?

3 Next week my uncle ______ (take) me out.

4 Jim ______ (not want) to play the guitar now.

5 Oh, no! The cat ______ (run) away.

6 You ______ (not know) Jane's niece.

## 6 Write the past simple of these verbs.

| | | | |
|---|---|---|---|
| 1 study | ______ | 7 live | ______ |
| 2 run | ______ | 8 sell | ______ |
| 3 be | ______ | 9 buy | ______ |
| 4 enjoy | ______ | 10 have | ______ |
| 5 come | ______ | 11 pay | ______ |
| 6 stop | ______ | 12 hurt | ______ |

## 7 Complete the short answers.

1 Is your grandma coming next week? No, ______.

2 Do you like your new house? Yes, ______.

3 Are we playing football this afternoon? Yes, ______.

4 Did your cousins visit you last summer? No, ______.

5 Did your mum save money? Yes, ______.

6 Is your brother buying a houseboat? No, ______.

## 8 Complete the paragraph with the present simple, the present continuous or the past simple of the verbs in brackets.

I'm really excited. Tomorrow we (1) ______ (move) into our new house. It (2) ______ (be) big – it (3) ______ (have got) four bedrooms. I (4) ______ (love) my new bedroom – it's green and white and very modern. Last week we (5) ______ (go) shopping for new furniture. My mum (6) ______ (buy) me a fantastic green and white bed. Yesterday we (7) ______ (clean) the house. Tonight we (8) ______ (stay) at my grandparents' house but tomorrow I can sleep in my new bed for the first time!

## Song TR: 2.13

We've got a new house and we mustn't be lazy!
We can't waste any time!
There's lots of work for me.
The house is very dirty!
It just looks awful, you see!
I pick up the rubbish and clean up carefully.

We've got a new house and there's so much to do!
We can't waste any time!
I've got some work for you.
Please clean the fridge and oven, the shower and the sink.
Pass the vacuum cleaner, too.
Oh, what do you think?

We're cleaning and we're working.
And it isn't much fun.
But as soon as we finish, we're playing in the sun.
Let's enjoy an afternoon in the park.
We'll only go home after it's dark.

We're at our new house and now it's clean.
It looks better than we've ever seen.
We worked so hard and now we're done.
We played outside, out in the sun.

Now we're in our new home, all clean and tidy.
We're having a great time, and we're all so happy!

# Video

## 1 BEFORE YOU WATCH

**Who does it? Tick P for *Penguins*, H for *Humans*, or B for *Both*.**

| | P | H | B |
|---|---|---|---|
| 1 Protect their young from danger. | ___ | ___ | ___ |
| 2 Hunt for food. | ___ | ___ | ___ |
| 3 Go to the shops for food. | ___ | ___ | ___ |
| 4 Feed their young. | ___ | ___ | ___ |
| 5 Cook food before eating it. | ___ | ___ | ___ |

**Now talk about what your parents do to take care of you.**

My dad makes delicious dinners!

My mum helps me with my maths homework!

## 2 WORDS TO KNOW

**Match the words to the pictures.**

dive chick wait chirp

___

___

___

___

## 3 WHILE YOU WATCH

**Circle the things that you can see in the video.**

| ice | penguins | fish |
|---|---|---|
| whales | sea | sand |
| snow | | |

## 4 AFTER YOU WATCH

**Answer the questions with 'Yes' or 'No'.**

1 Can the penguin chicks hear their parents chirp? ________

2 Can the penguin parents hear their chicks chirp? ________

3 Can the penguin chicks dive into the sea to catch food? ________

4 Do penguins eat fish? ________

5 Can the penguin chicks stay by themselves? ________

## 5 WATCH AGAIN

**How do you keep in touch with your parents when you're not together? Talk about it.**

I call my mum on my mobile phone after school to tell her that I'm walking home.

My parents and I leave notes for each other on the fridge.

# 3 Try Something New

Freefalling over Perris, California

**1** **Where are these people?**

- [ ] in the sky
- [ ] in the forest
- [ ] in the mountains

# Lesson 1

**1** **Listen. Listen and repeat.** TR: 3.1

deep

dive

equipment

explore

hobby

sure
wrong

**2** **Listen and read.** TR: 3.2

# Are You Ready to Explore the Sea?

**Scuba diving might be the hobby for you.**

## What were you doing last weekend?

Maybe you were reading a book or playing video games. These are good **hobbies**, but are you really seeing the world from your sofa? Why not try something new? It's time to get out and **explore**!

Take up an exciting hobby – scuba diving! You can be up close with all the beautiful underwater plants and animals. It's good exercise and great fun. But it can be dangerous. Before you **dive**, you must learn what to do to stay safe.

Midtown Scuba can help. In our one-week training programme, you learn:

- what **equipment** you need to stay safe
- how to turn on and use the equipment
- how to move around safely in **deep** waters
- what to do if something goes **wrong**

You want to be **sure** you're safe underwater! Make the right choice and call Midtown Scuba today!

**3** **Complete the words. Then match.**

1 w___ ___ ___ ___
2 h ___ ___ ___ ___
3 ___ ___ v ___
4 ___ x ___ ___ ___ ___ ___
5 d ___ ___ ___

a Go head-first into water
b Travel and learn about a new place
c What you do in your free time
d Incorrect
e For example, 4 m. (12 ft.) underwater

**4** **Read and complete the sentences.**

1 When scuba diving, you can be close to ______________________.
2 Scuba diving is great fun and ______________________.
3 A bad thing about scuba diving is that it can be ______________________.
4 You need to learn ______________________.
5 Midtown Scuba teaches what ______________ ______________ and how ______________.
6 They also teach you what to do if something ______________________.

## GRAMMAR Past continuous

We use the past continuous to:

**a** talk about things that were happening at a particular time in the past.
*Last night we **were painting** pictures.*

**b** talk about two or more things that were happening at the same time in the past.
*At eight o'clock, my little sister **was drawing** and I **was reading** a book.*

**c** to set the scene of a story.
*It **was snowing** and we **were making** a snowman.*

**Time expressions**

| | |
|---|---|
| all day yesterday | last year |
| all morning | this morning |
| at 3 o'clock | at this time last week/year |
| last Thursday | from three o'clock till four |

**Affirmative**
I/he/she/it was walking
you/we/they were walking

**Negative**
I/he/she/it wasn't (was not) walking
you/we/they weren't (were not) walking

**Questions**
Was I/he/she/it walking?
Were you/we/they walking?

**Short answers**
Yes, I/he/she/it was.
Yes, we/you/they were.
No, I/he/she/it wasn't.
No, we/you/they weren't.

**5 Complete the sentences with the past continuous of the verbs in brackets.**

1 I ______________ (tell) Anna about my new hobby.
2 Yesterday morning, it ______________ (rain) but we ______________(dive) underwater.
3 The twins ______________ (not play) outside because it was cold.
4 The new scuba equipment ______________ (not work).
5 They ______________ (study) the scuba diving book.

**6 Listen. Listen and repeat.** TR: 3.3

| | |
|---|---|
| **end up** | Jon ended up staying at home last night. |
| **give up** | Don't give up. You're almost finished! |
| **take up** | I'm taking up the guitar. My lessons start tomorrow. |
| **try out** | Nora tried out scuba diving and she really liked it. |
| **turn on** | Turn on the computer so we can read about sharks. |
| **use up** | When scuba diving, you mustn't use up all the air in your tank. |

**7 Complete the sentences with words from Activity 6.**

1 It's dark! Please ______________ the light.
2 I ______________! I can't play this game.
3 Can I ______________ your new skiing equipment?
4 Be careful! You don't want to ______________ with no air in your tank!
5 Why don't you start a new hobby? You can ______________ swimming.

**8 Listen. Tick T for *True* or F for *False*.** TR: 3.4

1 Anita had a great evening yesterday. T F
2 Anita was listening to music and helping her father. T F
3 Sara was also listening to music. T F
4 Raul was having dinner with Anita's family. T F

**9 Ask and answer these questions with your partner.**

1 What were you doing on Saturday afternoon?
2 What were your parents doing before school?
3 What was your teacher doing before class?

**10 Write four sentences about what you were doing at this time last week.**

# Lesson 2

**1** **Listen. Listen and repeat.** TR: 3.5

hill

pull

rope

slide

trick

show off

**2** **Listen and read.** TR: 3.6

**Guess what!** *Because of his red hair and his cool tricks, Shaun White got the name 'The Flying Tomato'.*

People around the world enjoy snowboarding because it's such an exciting sport! Snowboarders **slide** down a **hill**, like skiers do. But snowboarders go down on a single board, not with a ski on each foot.

Skiing is an old sport – people were using skis in the 1200s. But snowboarding is much newer. In 1965, a man named Sherman Poppen was trying to think of a way to take his daughters skiing with him. He put two skis together for his daughters to stand on. Then, he **pulled** them with a **rope**. They were having so much fun! So, Poppen worked on making a snowboard. His wife called the new activity *snurfing*, combining the words *snow* and *surfing*. Poppen sold his snurfer to a toy company, and snowboarding was born!

Snowboarding was getting more popular in the 1980s and 1990s, and it became an Olympic sport in 1998. American snowboarder Shaun White has won two Olympic gold medals for snowboarding. He's one of the most famous snowboarders in the world. Shaun was snowboarding when he was seven!

In this photo, Shaun is **showing off** a cool **trick**. Can you do this? Maybe not, but think about trying snowboarding as a hobby. With a helmet, goggles, a board, a big hill and lots of snow, you're sure to have fun!

**3** **Answer the questions.**

1 How are snowboarding and skiing different?
2 Why did Sherman Poppen make a snowboard?
3 When did Shaun White begin snowboarding?
4 What must you have to snowboard?

**4** **Complete the sentences with words from Activity 1.**

1 My dog is strong. It can ____________ me along when we walk.
2 You can ____________ down the hill in your sledge.
3 I'm tired from walking up this ____________.
4 Let's fasten the boat with this ____________.
5 Jana wants to ____________ her new computer to everyone.

## GRAMMAR Past simple and past continuous

We can use the past simple and the past continuous in the same sentence to:

**a** show one past action interrupted another one.
*I **was watching** a film when I **heard** the doorbell.*

**b** tell a story in the past.
*The divers **were taking** photos underwater when a shark **swam** by.*

We usually use *when* and *while* to connect the two actions. We use *when* before the past simple and *while* before the past continuous.

*We were playing football **when** it **started** to rain.*

*I had a brilliant idea **while** I **was watching** television.*

**5 Listen. Listen and repeat.** TR: 3.7

| | |
|---|---|
| **bored** | I'm really bored with this film. |
| **boring** | I went to sleep during that boring film. |
| **excited** | Are you excited to go diving? |
| **exciting** | Scuba diving is an exciting sport. |
| **interested** | Naomi is interested in this book. |
| **interesting** | This is a very interesting book. |
| **relaxed** | Mum feels relaxed after work. |
| **relaxing** | A hot bath can be very relaxing. |
| **tired** | Uncle Tao was snowboarding all afternoon. Now, he's tired. |
| **tiring** | Snowboarding is very tiring. |

**6 Read and circle the correct word.**

1 Reading a good book is **relaxed** / **relaxing**.

2 Are you **excited** / **exciting** about skiing?

3 Joao and Paula were swimming all morning. Now they're **tired** / **tiring**.

4 The students aren't **interested** / **interesting** in the lesson.

5 You must try out scuba diving. It isn't **bored** / **boring** at all!

**7 Complete the sentences.**

1 What ________ (you / do) when I ________ (call) you this morning?

2 I ________ (get) tired while I ________ (swim).

3 ________ (Luis / yawn) when the film ________ (start)?

4 The music ________ (not stop) while they ________ (dance) at the party.

5 The boy ________ (show off) when he ________ (fall in) the water.

**8 Listen and write.** TR: 3.8

Adam Lena Sasha Erik Tom

### SOUNDS OF ENGLISH TR: 3.9

**A** Read these pairs of words aloud, paying attention to the letters in red. How do they change when an **e** comes at the end of the word?

| | | | |
|---|---|---|---|
| Tim | time | fin | fine |
| hop | hope | hat | hate |

**B** Now read these words aloud, then listen and check your answers.

| | |
|---|---|
| slid | slide |
| can | cane |
| pin | pine |

# Lesson 3

**1** **Listen and read Kyra's blog. How have her pastimes changed?** TR: 3.10

kyrasblog.com

## Kyra's Blog

My teacher asked us to think about how our lives changed in five years, so I decided to blog about it. Five years ago, I was nine. I had a lot of free time. I used to play with my toys every day after school. I also used to play board games with my friends. Now that I'm fourteen, things are different. I don't like to play with toys, of course! I have a lot of homework and I can't do many fun things. For example, these days I don't watch TV very often. I used to watch TV for about two hours every day. That was a lot of TV! Now I go swimming every week. When I was nine, I didn't use to swim at all. I used to play football for exercise, and I used to play video games. But now, I know how to code. I'm learning how to make my own video games. Next week, I'm going to post a link for you to try out my game, Robot Round-Up. It's super fun!

So, my free time is very different, but there are some things that I still do. For example, I used to go ice-skating at the weekend, and I still do. I also used to read before bed, and I never stopped reading. But now, I'm reading my history books for school, not my favourite story books. And of course, when I was nine, I didn't use to have a blog. Now, I blog all the time! What about you? How is your life different from five years ago? Write your comments below.

**COMMENTS**

byronjm

Great post, Kyra! It looks like you're doing more interesting things than you used to do. I am learning to scuba dive now. When I was nine, I used to go swimming in the pool. Scuba diving is very different from swimming, but I think it's much more fun!

**2** **Re-read Kyra's blog. Write five things she used to do, and five things she does now.**

| Then | Now |
|---|---|
| | |

### SAY IT LIKE THIS!

**Talking about free time**

What do you do in your free time?
*I play chess/football. I go swimming/running.*

Do you like/love +*ing*?
*Do you* ***like riding*** *your bike/****watching*** *TV?*

Yes, I like/love +*ing*.
*Yes, I* ***love ice skating****.*

I hate/can't stand +*ing*
*No, I* ***can't stand drawing****.*

I started/stopped + *ing*
*I* ***started painting*** *when I was ten.*

**Talk about free time with your partner.**

## GRAMMAR Used to

We use **used to** to talk about:

**a** actions that happened often in the past but don't happen now.
*We **used to go** to the gym every day.*

**b** states that existed in the past but don't exist now.
*I **used to love** skiing but now I think it's boring.*

When we use a negative, we say **didn't use to**.
*Dad **didn't use to** cook very often.*

We use a bare infinitive after **used to**.

**Affirmative**
I/he/she/it/you/we/they used to play

**Negative**
I/he/she/it/you/we/they didn't use to play

**Question**
Did I/he/she/it/you/we/they use to play … ?

**Short answers**
Yes, I/he/she it/we/you/they did.
No, I/he/she it/we/you/they didn't.

### 3 Write sentences to say what Dan used to or didn't use to do/be.

1 be good at / maths

______________________________

2 collect / stamps

______________________________

3 watch / TV

______________________________

## WRITING Writing stories

### A Read about the tenses we usually use to write stories.

We often use the past simple and the past continuous to write stories.

We set the scene of a story with a sentence which has two verbs in the past continuous. We link the two halves of the sentence with **and**.
*It **was raining and** the boys **were playing** football.*

We can also use the past simple and the past continuous together in a story. We use **when** before the past simple and **while** before the past continuous.
*The boys were watching TV **when it happened**.*
*It happened **while** the boys **were watching** TV.*

### B Complete the sentences with and, when or while.

1 George was playing chess the ______________ the phone rang.

2 I fell in the water ______________ I was walking on the bridge.

3 It was a fantastic day. The snow was falling ______________ the boys were skiing.

### C Read the story and circle the correct words.

We were skiing in the mountains **and / when** we were having a great time. On the second day of our trip, something very interesting happened. We were putting our skis on **when / while** I saw a little white rabbit. The rabbit was sitting very still **when / and** it was difficult to see him in the snow.

Ten minutes later, I was skiing down the hill **and / while** I saw the rabbit again. I was trying to move out of his way **when / while** I fell over. **While / When** I was getting back up, the rabbit came nearer to me. He put his nose right on my hand, as if he was caring for me. Happy that I was OK, he ran away.

### D Write a story about something that happened in your free time.

**Paragraph 1** Set the scene. When and where did the story happen?

**Paragraph 2** Say what happened.

**Paragraph 3** Say how the story ended.

### E Remember to use and, when and while correctly in the sentences which use the past continuous and the past simple.

4

# Food and Drink

Candyfloss in the Zócalo, Mexico City, Mexico

**1 How does the food in the photo taste?**

- ☐ spicy
- ☐ salty
- ☐ sweet

# Lesson 1

| Hang on! | have got no idea | I don't believe it. |
|---|---|---|
| have a snack | Hurry up! | |

**1** **Listen. Listen and repeat.** TR: 4.1

**2** **Listen and read.** TR: 4.2

Elena: Let's go and eat. There's a huge breakfast buffet in the hotel lobby.

Julio: OK. **Hang on!** I'm brushing my teeth.

Elena: **Hurry up!** I can't wait. I'm so hungry.

[*At the buffet*]

Julio: Wow, look at all this food! **I don't believe it!** How much can we take?

Elena: We can take as much as we want. Look! Those eggs with tomato sauce look great.

Julio: Yes, I'm having some tortillas with my eggs. That's a real Mexican breakfast.

Elena: Yes, but don't take too many tortillas. There's a lot of food. You'll be full!

Julio: That's true. I want some fruit, too.

Elena: Yes, and try a little of this bread. It smells great.

Julio: OK. And look at this. What is it?

Elena: **I've got no idea!**

Waiter: Excuse me. Those are *frijoles* – fried beans. They're delicious. You must try them! Can I bring you some juice?

Elena: Yes, please. I'll have a mango juice.

Julio: And I'll have a little orange juice.

[*After breakfast*]

Elena: Wow! This breakfast was the best. But, I ate too much. I'm really full.

Julio: Not me. The food in Mexico is so good, I'll be ready to **have a snack** soon.

**3** **Circle the best response.**

1 You win a contest. You say:
 a Hurry up! b I don't believe it!

2 Your brother asks how a spider got into your house. You say:
 a I don't believe it! b I've got no idea.

3 You're late for school. Your mum says:
 a Get dressed! Hurry up!
 b Hang on! I'm making breakfast.

4 You're reading a good book and your sister wants you to play with her. You say:
 a Hang on! b I've got no idea.

5 Your friend is hungry. You say:
 a I've got no idea. b Here, have a snack.

**4** **Answer the questions.**

1 Where are Julio and Elena?

2 Why does Elena say, 'Hurry up!'?

3 What foods do they take from the buffet?

4 What does the waiter say is delicious?

5 What does the waiter bring them?

6 Who wants to eat more at the end?

## 5 Listen. Listen and repeat. TR: 4.3

| | |
|---|---|
| **altogether** | The sandwich and fizzy drink cost ten euros altogether. |
| **disgusting** | That fish was sitting out all afternoon. It looks disgusting. |
| **delicious** | May I please have more cake? It's delicious. |
| **full** | We ate a lot of food and now we're full. |
| **thirsty** | If you're thirsty, I'll bring you some water. |

## 6 Match.

1 I need some water.
2 The sandwich is $4 and the juice is $1.
3 That fruit smells awful!
4 That's really tasty!
5 I can't eat any more.

a It's disgusting.
b I'm full.
c I'm thirsty.
d It's delicious.
e It's $5 altogether.

### GRAMMAR Much, many

We use **much** and **many** to describe quantities. We use **much** in negative sentences and questions with uncountable nouns and we use **many** in affirmative and negative sentences and questions with plural countable nouns.

*Guy hasn't got **much** lemonade.*

*There aren't **many** apples in the bowl.*

We use **How much/many … ?** to ask about quantities of countable and uncountable things.

***How much** money have you got?*

***How many** bananas did you eat?*

## 7 Circle the correct words.

1 How **much** / **many** time have we got before dinner?
2 How **much** / **many** are those potatoes?
3 There aren't **much** / **many** tins of tomatoes.
4 There isn't **much** / **many** lemonade in the bottle.
5 Do we need **much** / **many** eggs?
6 How **much** / **many** sandwiches do we need for the picnic?

### GRAMMAR A lot of, lots of, a few, a little

We use **a lot of** or **lots of** with countable and uncountable nouns in affirmative and negative sentences and questions.

*There are **a lot of** bananas on that tree.*

*There is **lots of** water in the jug.*

We use **a few** with countable nouns in affirmative sentences and questions.

*Robbie ate **a few** crisps.*

We use **a little** with uncountable nouns in affirmative sentences and questions.

*Is there **a little** milk in the fridge?*

## 8 Write a little, a few or a lot of.

1 I'm full because I had ______ food for dinner.
2 I've got just ______ milk in my tea.
3 We've got ______ people coming to the show tomorrow. We need more chairs.
4 You can only have ______ sweets. They aren't good for you.

## 9 Complete the dialogue between the shopkeeper (S) and the woman (W). Then, listen and check your answers. TR: 4.4

**S:** Good morning.
**W:** Hello. I need (1) ______ eggs. Have you got any? I need six.
**S:** Of course. Here you are, six eggs.
**W:** Can you also give me three bottles of lemonade? We drink (2) ______ lemonade. Oh, and (3) ______ vanilla ice cream, too. And (4) ______ of those delicious doughnuts.
**S:** (5) ______ doughnuts?
**W:** Four, please.
**S:** Here you are!
**W:** Thank you. (6) ______ is that altogether?
**S:** That's eleven euros, please.

## 10 Work with a partner and practise the dialogue in Activity 9. Then role-play going shopping for food with your own dialogue.

## 11 Write down a dialogue like the one in the Activity 9. In your dialogue, the customer must ask for four items.

# Lesson 2

**1** Listen. Listen and repeat. TR: 4.5

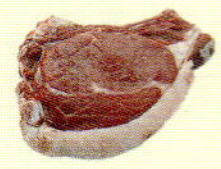
meat

pot

raw

sauce

seafood

soup

healthy

**2** Listen and read. TR: 4.6

You can get Chinese food almost anywhere in the world. And it seems like everybody has got one Chinese dish that they think is delicious, like Peking duck or wonton **soup**. But to really enjoy traditional Chinese food, you must travel to China.

With 1.4 billion people, China has the world's largest population. And with so many people, there are thousands of different dishes to try. Many of China's most popular dishes come from the Sichuan region. But if you visit that region of China, don't have a familiar dish. Try a hot-**pot** dinner instead. And if you go, be sure to bring your friends and family – you get lots of food!

At a hot-pot restaurant in Sichuan, the food comes out **raw**. You cook it yourself at the table. You get a large bowl of boiling soup, noodles, vegetables and raw **meat** or **seafood**. You add these foods to the pot, one at a time. Then, you mix it with a spoon or chopsticks. The food cooks in front of you. When it's finished, you can dip it in any of the **sauces** you have on the table. Then, eat it and enjoy!

A hot-pot dinner is delicious, **healthy** and fun to make. At a hot-pot restaurant, everybody is a chef!

**Guess what!** You can tell that your hot-pot food is cooked when it floats to the top of your bowl.

**3** Read and tick T for *True* or F for *False*.

1 Peking duck is a dish you can get around the world. T F

2 Few people around the world think Chinese food is delicious. T F

3 More people live in China than in any other country. T F

4 Hot pot is the only popular dish from the Sichuan region. T F

5 You cook your own food at a hot-pot restaurant. T F

**4** Write the word for each definition.

1 ________ Something you use to boil water

2 ________ Anything that's good for your body

3 ________ Not cooked

4 ________ Something that you put on food to make it tastier

5 ________ A hot dish that often has meat and noodles

## 5 Listen. Listen and repeat. TR: 4.7

add

boil

chop

fry

mix

slice

## 6 Complete the recipe with words from Activity 5.

1 __________ the onions into small pieces.

2 __________ the vegetables in oil.

3 __________ the rice for 15 minutes.

4 __________ the onions to the rice.

5 __________ the onions and the rice together.

6 __________ a tomato to put on the rice.

### GRAMMAR Some, any, every, no

We use **some** and **any** when it isn't important how many people, things or places there are. We use **some** for affirmative sentences and **any** for negative sentences and questions.

*I want **some** cakes, please.*

*There aren't **any** people at the table.*

We use **every** when we talk about all people, things or places. It has a positive meaning and we use it with a singular verb form.

***Every** restaurant in town is expensive.*

We use **no** when we talk about no person, thing or place. **No** has a negative meaning but we use it with an affirmative verb form.

*There were **no** sauces on the table.*

## 7 Write some, any, every or no.

1 I didn't get ______________ noodles.

2 Bring ______________ beans from the garden.

3 There's ______________ meat in the fridge. Please buy some.

4 Is there ______________ sugar in my tea?

5 We added ______________ food on the table to the hot pot.

### GRAMMAR Indefinite pronouns

We use **somebody**, **something** and **somewhere** to talk about one person, thing or place in affirmative sentences.

***Somebody** ate my dinner.*

We use **anybody**, **anything** and **anywhere** to talk about one person, thing or place in negative sentences and questions.

*Is there **anything** for lunch? I'm really hungry.*

We use **everybody**, **everything** and **everywhere** to talk about all people, things or places but we use them with a singular verb form.

*I looked **everywhere**, but I didn't find the eggs.*

We use **nobody**, **nothing** and **nowhere** to talk about no person, thing or place. We use an affirmative verb with these words but the meaning of the sentence is negative.

*We're hungry because we had **nothing** for lunch.*

## 8 Match.

| | |
|---|---|
| 1 Waiter! There's | a everybody in the room. |
| 2 James doesn't want | b nobody can come. |
| 3 Give a cake to | c anything for lunch. |
| 4 They asked three people for dinner but | d something in my soup! |

## 9 Listen. Number the pictures in order. TR: 4.8

☐ 
☐ 
☐ 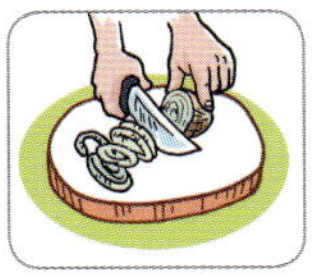
☐ 
☐ 
☐ 

### SOUNDS OF ENGLISH TR: 4.9

**A** Say. What sound do the red letters make?

b**ee** hon**ey** t**ea**

**B** Listen and repeat the rhyme.

I saw a bee asleep in a tree. I said 'Wake up, Mrs Bee, here is some money. Bring me some honey for my cup of tea.'
'I make honey,' said she. 'I don't take money. And I'm asleep, can't you see?'

# Lesson 3

**1 Listen and read the recipe for Spicy Hot Chocolate. Do you want to try it? Why or why not?** TR: 4.10

cookscorner.com

Cook's Corner

Search

## Spicy Hot Chocolate

★★★★★

This is a delicious hot chocolate recipe that's also a little spicy. It will warm you up on a cold day! Makes four servings.

**You need:**

- 50 g white sugar
- 50 g cocoa powder
- 2 tablespoons chilli powder
- 230 ml boiling water
- 1 red chilli pepper, sliced thinly
- 450 ml milk

**How to make Spicy Hot Chocolate:**

1 Put the sugar, cocoa powder and chilli powder in a pan.
2 Heat the pan gently.
3 Add the water and pepper slices and mix together.
4 Boil everything together for five minutes. Then, turn heat down.
5 Add the milk and heat until it is warm.
6 Remove the pepper slices with a spoon.
7 Pour into mugs and serve. You can even put a little cocoa powder on top, if you want.

**2 Circle the correct words.**

1 The recipe is for hot chocolate that's a little **spicy** / **salty**.
2 One ingredient that's not in the recipe is **eggs** / **sugar**.
3 The **first** / **second** step in the recipe is to heat the pan.
4 You must **boil** / **fry** the water, sugar, powders and pepper together.
5 Before you serve, you must **add** / **remove** the pepper slices.
6 You can put **cocoa powder** / **sliced peppers** on top if you want.

**SAY IT LIKE THIS!**

**What's for dinner?**

How about/What about + *-ing*
Would you like … ?
***How about*** *cooking seafood?*
***Would you like*** *fish and chips?*
*Yes, that's a good idea.*
*No, I'd like rice/soup for dinner.*

**Work with a partner. Take it in turns to use How about … ?, What about … ? and Would you like … ? to make and respond to suggestions for dinner.**

## 3 Listen to Tomas talking about the food the people in his family like and dislike. Then complete the table. TR: 4.11

| | Likes | Doesn't like |
|---|---|---|
| Ana | prawns | |
| Javi | honey | |
| Susana | | fried eggs |
| Tomas | | cakes |

## 4 Look again at the table in Activity 3. Then work with a partner and take it in turns to say what the people think of the food. Use these words.

awful delicious disgusting tasty

Ana thinks prawns are tasty.

## 5 Now work with a partner and take it in turns to say what you think of these foods. Use the words from Activity 4.

1 

2 

3 

4 

5 

6 

7 

8 

## WRITING Letters and emails

### A We use these phrases when we send letters and emails to our friends and family.

Dear …
How are you?
Bye for now!
Love from …

### B Complete the email with the phrases from Activity A.

**Email**

(1) ________ Lucinda,

Hi! (2) ________ I'm fine! I'm sending a recipe for my mum's tomato fondue. I hope you like it!

**Mum's Tomato Fondue**

*You need:*

*one onion*
*one tin of tomatoes*
*200 g cheese*

First, chop the onion and fry it in a frying pan. Then add the tomatoes and the cheese. Mix everything together and cook for five minutes. Last of all, dip squares of bread into the tomato and cheese sauce and enjoy your meal!

I hope you like it! (3) ________

(4) ________ Kendra

### C Write an email to a friend to share an easy recipe. Use the plan below to help you.

**Begin like this:**
Dear ________

**Answer the questions:**
What's the name of your dish?
What ingredients do you need?
What do you do first?
Then what do you do?
What do you do last of all?

**Finish like this:**
Love from ________

### D Read your email and check that it includes all the phrases from Part A and **First**, **Then** and **Last of all**.

# Review

## 1 Label the photos.

______________

______________

______________

______________

______________

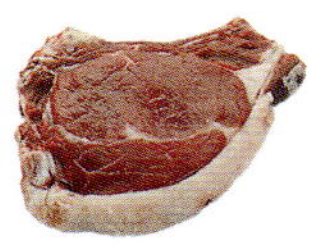

______________

## 2 Circle the odd one out.

| | | | |
|---|---|---|---|
| 1 | interesting | exciting | boring |
| 2 | raw | boil | fry |
| 3 | chop | pull | slice |
| 4 | show off | trick | chop |
| 5 | I've got no idea. | I'm thirsty. | I'm full. |
| 6 | hobby | delicious | equipment |

## 3 Replace the words in bold with synonyms.

disgusting dive raw taking up wrong

1 That's **not right**. ______________

2 The fish was **not cooked**. ______________

3 Fried pasta is **not tasty at all**. ______________

4 She's **trying out** a new hobby. ______________

5 Let's **jump head-first** into the pool. ______________

## 4 Choose the correct answers.

1 Beto was _____ on his new boat when he fell into the sea.
  a showing off b taking up c giving up

2 Be careful! This water is very _____.
  a relaxing b deep c raw

3 Maria felt very _____ and she fell asleep.
  a boring b tiring c bored

4 Are you _____ that insect isn't dangerous?
  a relaxed b sure c full

5 I'm _____. I don't want to eat any more.
  a healthy b full c thirsty

## 5 Complete the paragraph with the past simple or the past continuous of the verbs in brackets.

Last week I (1) ______________ (go) to a new water park with some friends. The sun (2) ______________ (shine) and it was really hot. We (3) ______________ (stand) next to the water slide when some kids (4) ______________ (say) something mean to us. Then my friend (5) ______________ (fall) in the water with his clothes on. While he (6) ______________ (get) out, we (7) ______________ (see) that his hat was still in the water! We used a long stick to get it out.

## 6 Circle the correct words.

1 Can I have **a few** / **a little** fried rice, please?

2 I didn't buy **anything** / **nothing** at the market.

3 I don't watch TV because I don't have **much** / **many** free time.

4 There is **a lot of** / **a few** food here – we can't eat all of it!

5 **Are there** / **Is there** many people in the restaurant?

6 How **many** / **much** hobbies have you got?

7 Where **is** / **are** everybody?

8 We didn't play the game because **nothing** / **nobody** knew how to play.

## 7 Complete the sentences with **when** or **while**.

1 What were you eating ______________ you felt sick?

2 Sophie watched me ______________ I was sliding down the hill.

3 ______________ Emilio was cooking, I made the salad.

4 ______________ the accident happened, was it raining?

## 8 Complete the sentences with **use** or **used**.

1 I ______________ to read a lot of comics but now I like writing my blog.

2 We didn't ______________ to enjoy snowboarding but we love it now.

3 A few years ago my brother ______________ to eat only cakes and sweets.

4 Did you ______________ to have scuba diving lessons once or twice a week?

## 9 Fill in the blanks with words that start with **some**, **any**, **every** or **no**.

1 Hiro's house is ______________ near here, but I'm not sure where.

2 Did ______________ arrive at the party on time? Or was ______________ late?

3 This food is too spicy. There are hot chilli peppers in ______________ on the plate.

4 There's ______________ time to waste. Hurry up!

5 We haven't got ______________ money to go to the hot-pot restaurant. We'll have to cook ______________ at home.

## 10 Answer the questions.

1 What were you doing last night?

2 How much free time do you have each day? What do you do with it?

3 How many sweets do you eat in a week?

4 Does anybody you know have an interesting hobby? What is it?

## Song TR: 4.12

Oh, what's your hobby?
What do you like to do?
Do you like to do the same old thing
or try out something new?
Go surfing or snowboarding,
scuba diving, too.
Cooking, singing or painting,
it's all up to you!

Jane used to be bored every afternoon.
She had no idea what to do in her room.
Then one day while she was watching TV,
She saw a programme on caring for bees.
Now Jane's got an exciting new hobby:
Beekeeping and collecting bees' honey.

Oh, what's your hobby?
What do you like to do?
Do you like to do the same old thing
or try out something new?
Go surfing or snowboarding,
scuba diving, too.
Cooking, singing or painting,
it's all up to you!

Rick used to spend hours just watching TV.
Then one day he said, 'Learning coding's
for me!'
He studied and worked on a laptop
he bought.
He created and programmed his own robot.
Now Rick teaches coding to children
after school.
He's found a way to be helpful and it's
really cool!

Oh, what's your hobby?
What do you like to do?
It's up to you to try something new.
Yes, it's up to you to try something new!

# Video

**1** BEFORE YOU WATCH

**What do you eat for lunch? Circle.**

| | |
|---|---|
| pizza | yoghurt |
| lemonade | nuts |
| a sandwich | fruit |

At lunch, I eat ______________________.

**Now talk about your favourite food to eat for lunch.**

I love it when I have pizza for lunch.

I like it when I get to eat crisps with my sandwich.

**2** WORDS TO KNOW

**Match the words to the pictures.**

cauliflower food waste consume reject

______________

______________

______________

______________

## 3 WHILE YOU WATCH

**What actions can you see people doing in the video?**

These people are:

chopping vegetables
boiling water
mixing vegetable curry
slicing carrots
carrying boxes of vegetables
cooking meat
shopping at the market

## 4 AFTER YOU WATCH

**Tick T for *True* or F for *False*.**

1 People can't eat 'ugly' food. T F

2 The cooks and volunteers are making enough food for 500 people. T F

3 People in America waste a lot of food every year. T F

4 Feeding people with 'ugly' food is a solution to food waste. T F

5 People won't buy 'ugly' food because it is the wrong shape or size. T F

## 5 WATCH AGAIN

**How can you reduce food waste? Talk about it.**

When I can't finish my lunch, I can have it for a snack later.

I can try to finish my lunch.

# 5 School and Beyond

Children doing fencing, Rome, Italy

**1 What are these children doing?**

- ☐ dancing
- ☐ eating
- ☐ learning
- ☐ smiling

# Lesson 1

**1** **Listen. Listen and repeat.** TR: 5.1

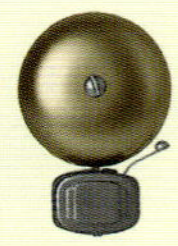

bell

canteen

magazine

sweatshirt

break
term

**2** **Listen and read.** TR: 5.2

## HelpMe Hal

**ANSWERS YOUR QUESTIONS**

Dear HelpMe Hal,

I've just moved to Berlin, and this is my first **term** at Handel School. I've been at the school two weeks, and I haven't met any new friends. I have tried to talk to classmates after the **bell** rings at the end of the lessons, but nobody says much to me at all. Well, one person did. She told me that I can't wear a **sweatshirt** over my uniform. I'm really friendly, and want to meet people. I've never changed schools before. I don't know what to do. Please help!

Lonely Lea

HelpMe HAL!

Dear Lonely Lea,

Congratulations! You've taken your first step. Writing a letter to the school **magazine** is a great thing to do. Now, people will know that there's a super-friendly new student. Here are some ideas for making friends. First, don't talk to friends after the bell rings. Most people must move quickly to their next lesson. It's not you – people haven't got the time to talk. Instead, ask to sit with classmates at lunch, in the **canteen**. You'll have more time. Or, go out into the playground during the **break**. Find people doing something that is interesting to you, and talk to them. You'll have friends in no time!

Good luck,

HelpMe Hal

**3** **Unscramble and match.**

1 mert ____________

2 neacent ____________

3 ekarb ____________

4 zagimean ____________

5 histtwears ____________

a Something you wear to keep warm

b Something you read

c The time in between lessons

d A part of the school year

e The place where students eat lunch

**4** **Read. Tick T for *True* and F for *False*.**

1 Lea has been at her school for two years. T F

2 Hal is new to Handel School. T F

3 Lea has worn a sweatshirt to school. T F

4 Lea has made lots of friends. T F

5 Hal tells Lea to talk to friends after the bell. T F

6 Lea can meet friends by talking to them in the canteen. T F

## 5 Listen. Listen and repeat. TR: 5.3

| | |
|---|---|
| **cheat** | Greta is cheating. She's looking at Jon's exam paper. |
| **fair** | It's not fair that only some students got homework. |
| **head teacher** | The head teacher must make sure that students are in class. |
| **strict** | Don't be late for Mr Jones's class – he's very strict! |
| **test** | Let's study for the maths test. |

## 6 Circle the correct words.

1 Let's study for our history **test** / **head teacher**.

2 Victor has talked to the **head teacher** / **magazine** about his school work.

3 Nobody talks in Mr Tran's class because he is so **fair** / **strict**.

4 Gil was **cheating** / **fair** on his English test, so the teacher made him start again.

### GRAMMAR Present perfect simple

We use the present perfect simple to say what:

**a** started in the past and is still happening.
*Sally's not at school. She**'s gone** to the dentist.*

**b** has just finished.
***I've just finished** my homework. Now, let's play!*

**c** happened in the past without saying when.
*The head teacher **has been** very busy this week.*

**d** happened in the past but affects the present.
*He**'s broken** his hand so he can't write.*

To form this tense, use *have* and the past participle of the main verb.

## 7 Complete the sentences with the present perfect simple of the verbs in brackets.

1 He ________________ (finish) the book.

2 I ________________ (learn) about Egypt.

3 They ________________ (have) English lessons before.

4 We ________________ (do) two tests today.

### GRAMMAR For, since, already, just, never

We use **for** to show a period of time and **since** to show when something started.

*I **have been** at this school **for** six months.*

*They **have been** in class 5B **since** the autumn.*

We use **already** to show a time before now and **just** to talk about a recent event.

*We**'ve already had** a maths test this week.*
***I've just had** a brilliant idea.*

We use **never** to talk about things that haven't happened so far. We use an affirmative verb with **never** but the meaning is negative.

***I've never had** a C in geography.*

## 8 Circle the correct words.

1 I've known my best friend **for** / **since** primary school.

2 I've **just** / **never** been to your school. Is it far?

3 Miss Tao has taught us **for** / **since** six years.

4 Alice is very clever. She has **already** / **never** passed the maths exam.

5 I've **just** / **since** met the new gym teacher.

6 Jason and Ben have **already** / **since** gone to school.

## 9 Listen and write the names. TR: 5.4

Ada Anders Ivan Hannah Lucy

## 10 Complete these sentences with a partner.

At school this week, I have already …
In class, I have just …
At school, I have never …

**Now tell the class what your partner said.**

## 11 Write down the three sentences you told the class about your partner in Activity 10.

# Lesson 2

**1** Listen. Listen and repeat. TR: 5.5

exam

nature reserve

discuss

friendship
in the wild
understanding

**2** Listen and read. TR: 5.6

Have you ever taken a school trip to a **nature reserve**? Well, one school in South Africa is actually *on* a nature reserve. The Southern Cross Boarding School, in Hoedspruit, sits on a 1,100 hectare (2,700 acre) nature reserve, with many different types of wildlife including giraffes, snakes and wild boars.

At Southern Cross, students work inside classrooms, just like you, but they also spend time learning **in the wild**. The school's teachers feel students need a deep **understanding** of the natural world so that they can care for it. Teachers take students outside during all types of lessons. For example, preschool students don't learn counting with a workbook. Instead, they go to the farm to count animals. In a language lesson, students **discuss** problems facing the plants and animals on the reserve. They work together to find the best solutions.

Southern Cross students also enjoy activities such as rock climbing, kayaking and horse riding. Their education isn't just about homework and **exams**. Students solve real-world problems, have fun and build **friendships** – all while learning to care for the Earth!

**Guess what!** To get to their lessons, Southern Cross students must walk on a path that's also used by the animals. Imagine saying 'Good morning!' to a passing wildebeest on the way to your morning lesson!

**3** **Change the words in bold to make the sentences true.**

1 The Southern Cross school is **in a village**.

2 Unlike most schools, students at this school spend lots of time **in a classroom**.

3 Teachers want students to have an understanding of **taking exams**.

4 Preschool students learn counting **with a workbook**.

5 In addition to lessons, students enjoy **studying and doing lots of homework**.

**4** **Complete the sentences with words from Activity 1.**

1 It takes time to build a ________________ with another person.

2 Let's ________________ the problems at our school to find good solutions.

3 Mr Lee is a great teacher. He's got a good ________________ of maths.

4 There's no hunting the animals on the ________________.

5 Did you study for the final ________________ in history?

## 5 Listen. Listen and repeat. TR: 5.7

| | |
|---|---|
| **boarding school** | Giselle goes to boarding school. She's home on holiday. |
| **education** | Mum says that a good education is more important than anything. |
| **marks** | Anya receives the highest marks of all the students in her class. |
| **report** | The teacher gave Victor a good report, saying he is kind. |
| **time off** | We get lots of time off from school: six weeks during the year. |

## 6 Match.

1 Mateo is packing his bag for
2 In her report, the teacher
3 He studied a lot for his final exam, so
4 We're on holiday in June and July and we've
5 In nature-based education

a got some time off in December, too.
b students work with plants and animals.
c his next term at boarding school.
d he got the highest marks.
e said she needed to study more.

### GRAMMAR Present perfect simple

**Negative**
I haven't (have not) eaten.
He/She/It hasn't (he/she/it has not) eaten.
We/You/They haven't (have not) eaten.

**Questions**
Have I eaten?
Has he/she/it eaten?
Have we/you/they eaten?

**Short answers**
Yes, I have. / No, I haven't.
Yes, he/she/it has. / No, he/she/it hasn't.
Yes, we/you/they have.
No, we/you/they haven't.

### SOUNDS OF ENGLISH TR: 5.8

A Say these pairs of words. Which sound starts each word in the left column?

| | | | |
|---|---|---|---|
| head | Ed | had | add |
| has | as | hold | old |

B Listen and repeat the rhyme.
*Happy old Ed held his hat on his head.*

### GRAMMAR Ever, yet

We use **ever** in questions to ask about things that have happened up to now. **Ever** comes before the past participle in the sentence.
*Have you* ***ever*** *been away on a school trip?*

We use **yet** with negatives and questions when we want to say *until now*. **Yet** comes at the end of the sentence.
*Have you cleaned the board* ***yet****?*
*I haven't studied for my exam* ***yet****.*

## 7 Complete the sentences.

1 We ______________ (not do) a spelling test yet this week.
2 ______________ ever ______________ (Mrs Smith / give) you bad marks?
3 I ______________ (not have) a bad report this year.
4 ______________ (you / finish) your project?
5 We ______________ (not learn) about the Amazon yet.

## 8 Match the questions with the short answers.

1 Has Lucy got her report yet?
2 Has Peter ever had bad marks?
3 Have they read this book yet?
4 Have you ever passed an exam?

a Yes, they have.
b No, she hasn't.
c No, he hasn't.
d Yes, I have.

## 9 Listen. Circle the correct words. TR: 5.9

1 **Mr Rogers** / **Miss Andrews** is away.
2 The class has done Exercise 5 on page **15** / **50**.
3 The class **has** / **has not** read the text on the next page.
4 **Isla** / **Henry** reads the article on elephants.

## 10 Work in pairs to talk about the following.

1 Have you had much time off school yet this year? When is your next holiday?
2 Have you earned high marks this year? In what classes?
3 Has your teacher given a report on you? What has he/she said about you?

# Lesson 3

**1** **Listen and read the interview for a the school paper. What does the reporter hope at the end?** TR: 5.10

## Who's new at school?

**This year, there are a lot of new teachers at school and today we are interviewing one of them, Mr Romero, the new French teacher.**

Angela: Mr Romero, why did you come to Silva Community School?

Mr R: Well, I was working in France but one day I saw an advert for this job on the Internet. I came back home, got the job and here I am!

Angela: So how long have you been teaching here?

Mr R: Let me see. Three months, I think. Yes, I moved here in the summer holidays and then we started lessons in September.

Angela: Have you ever taught in this town before?

Mr R: Yes, I have. I worked in a school in the town centre a few years ago. I love it here.

Angela: Have you taught in many other schools?

Mr R: No, I haven't. Just three: one in France and two here.

Angela: Have you met many new people since you came back?

Mr R: Yes, I have because it isn't a big town. Everyone knows everyone else. That's nice! My daughter Elsa has made lots of friends, too. And there are many people here we have known for a long time, because I'm from this town.

Angela: Well, it was nice talking to you, Mr Romero. I hope you don't give us too much homework!

**2** **Answer the questions.**

1 Where was Mr Romero working before he came to Silva Community School?
2 How long has he been in this town?
3 Where else in the town has Mr Romero worked?
4 How many schools has he taught in?
5 Has he met many new people?
6 Who has made lots of friends?

### SAY IT LIKE THIS!

**Talking about school**

Where do you go to school?
I go to school at ....
What is you favourite subject?
My favourite subject is ....
What are you good at?
I'm good at ....
Who is your favourite teacher?
My favourite teacher is ....

**Discuss these questions with a partner.**

## GRAMMAR Present perfect simple and *How long*

We can use **How long** with the present perfect simple to ask questions about the length of time something has happened.

***'How long have** you **lived** here?' 'Three years.'*

***'How long have** you **taught** French?' 'Two months.'*

**3 Write questions with the present perfect simple and How long.**

1 Sandra / teach German / ?

______

2 Petra and Raul / have tennis lessons / ?

______

3 she / be teacher / ?

______

4 you / know Myrna / ?

______

5 they / be at this school / ?

______

6 I / study / science / ?

______

7 the student / sleep / in class / ?

______

8 Miss Jones / work / at Golding School / ?

______

**4 Work in pairs. Discuss the questions.**

1 How long have you lived in this town?

2 How long have you known your best friend?

3 How long have you been at this school?

## WRITING Paragraphs

**A Read about paragraphs and topic sentences.**

A piece of writing consists of paragraphs, and each paragraph has got a different subject. The first or second sentence of a paragraph usually introduces this subject. This is called the topic sentence.

**B Read the email and underline the topic sentences in each paragraph.**

**Email**

Hi Sam,

How are you? I'm writing to tell you about my new school. There's a lot happening this week. I had a school trip yesterday, and I have a project. We've got a history test this afternoon and we've already had three this week! I've never done three tests in one week before!

I've just had lunch in the canteen. The food has been good this week. I had spaghetti today. It was delicious!

Why don't you come over to my house this weekend? You haven't seen my new computer yet. It's brilliant! You can have lunch with us. Let me know about the weekend!

Bye for now!

Kim

**C Write an email to a friend in another town about what you are doing at school this week. Use this plan to help you.**

| | |
|---|---|
| **Paragraph 1:** | How are you? I'm writing because … |
| **Paragraph 2:** | Say what is happening at school. |
| **Paragraph 3:** | Invite your friend to your house and say what you can do together. |
| **Paragraph 4:** | End the email. Bye for now! |

**D Read your email and check that the main paragraphs all contain a topic sentence.**

6

# Our Amazing Bodies

A boy doing a back flip off a tree stump, Calla Varcas, Majorca, Spain

**1** **Look at the photo. Say all the body parts you can see.**

# Lesson 1

**1** **Listen. Listen and repeat.** TR: 6.1

(catch a) cold

cough

sneeze

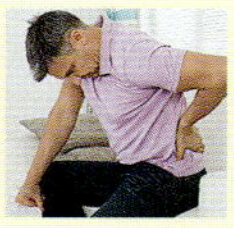
ache

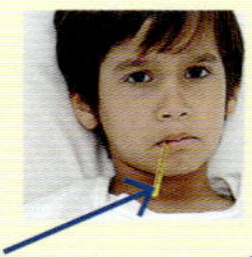
thermometer
temperature

earache
headache
stomach ache
toothache

**2** **Listen and read.** TR: 6.2

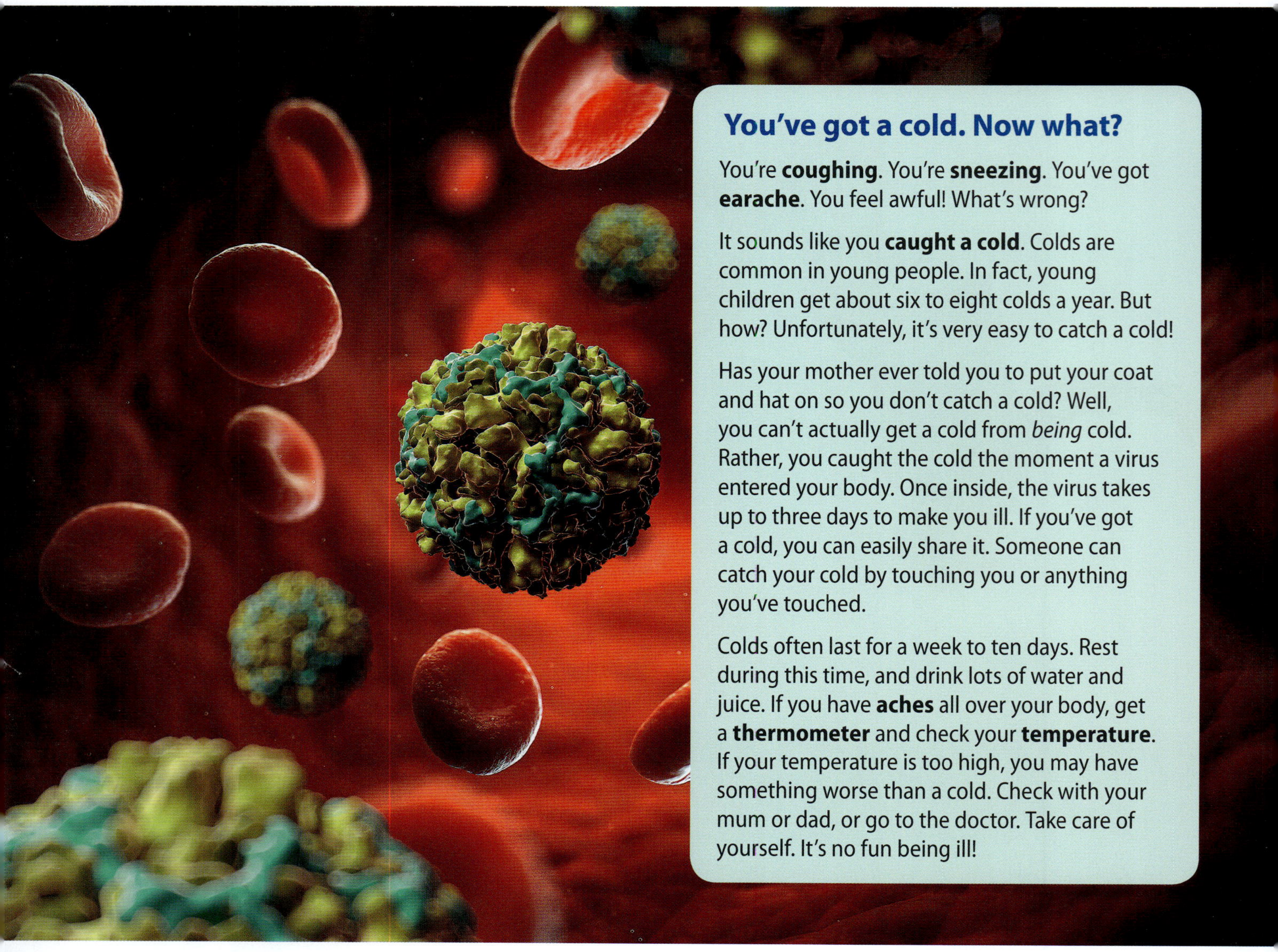

## You've got a cold. Now what?

You're **coughing**. You're **sneezing**. You've got **earache**. You feel awful! What's wrong?

It sounds like you **caught a cold**. Colds are common in young people. In fact, young children get about six to eight colds a year. But how? Unfortunately, it's very easy to catch a cold!

Has your mother ever told you to put your coat and hat on so you don't catch a cold? Well, you can't actually get a cold from *being* cold. Rather, you caught the cold the moment a virus entered your body. Once inside, the virus takes up to three days to make you ill. If you've got a cold, you can easily share it. Someone can catch your cold by touching you or anything you've touched.

Colds often last for a week to ten days. Rest during this time, and drink lots of water and juice. If you have **aches** all over your body, get a **thermometer** and check your **temperature**. If your temperature is too high, you may have something worse than a cold. Check with your mum or dad, or go to the doctor. Take care of yourself. It's no fun being ill!

**3** **Write.**

1 What you use to tell the temperature
t __ __ __ __ __ __ __ __ __ __

2 A bad feeling in your body a __ __ __

3 What comes with aches and a high temperature
f __ __ __ __

4 When air comes out of your nose and mouth
s __ __ __ __ __

5 You put your hand over your mouth to do this
c __ __ __ __

**4** **Read. Tick T for *True* and F for *False*.**

1 Coughing and sneezing are signs of a cold. T F

2 Young children get about six to eight colds in their life. T F

3 It's difficult to catch a cold. T F

4 You can get a cold if you don't wear the right clothing. T F

5 When a virus enters your body, you get ill straight away. T F

6 You can use a thermometer to check your temperature. T F

## GRAMMAR Past simple and present perfect simple

We use the past simple for:

**a** things that started and finished in the past.
*I **hurt** my elbow last night.*

**b** things that happened one after the other.
*I **opened** the door, **fell** on the floor and **hit** my head.*

**c** habits in the past.
*When I was a child, I **wore** socks in bed.*

**Time expressions for past simple:**
yesterday, last night/week/month/year, three days/a month/a year ago, in January/2014

We use the present perfect simple to talk about things that:

**a** started in the past and are still happening.
*My leg **has hurt** for three days.*

**b** have just finished.
*I**'ve just washed** my hands.*

**c** happened in the past but we don't say exactly when.
*He **has fallen off** the horse twice.*

**d** happened in the past but have a result which affects the present.
*I**'ve walked** all around the park, and now I'm tired.*

**Time expressions for present perfect simple:**
ever, never, already, just, for, since, yet

### 5 Circle the correct words.

1 Ow! I think you **have broken** / **broke** my nose!

2 **Did** / **Have** you cleaned your teeth yet?

3 I **fell off** / **have fallen off** a horse yesterday and hurt my elbow.

4 My stomach hurts because I **haven't eaten** / **didn't eat** since yesterday.

5 When she **lived** / **has lived** in Germany, she **broke** / **has broken** her ankle.

### 6 Listen. Listen and repeat. TR: 6.3

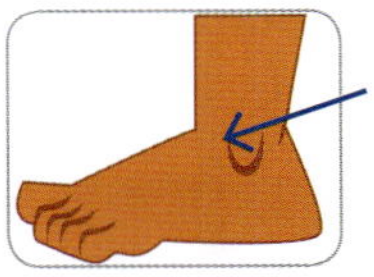
ankle

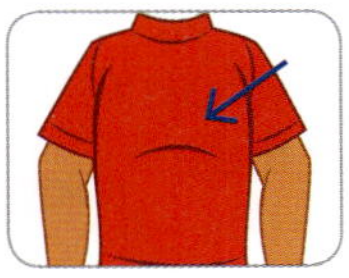
chest

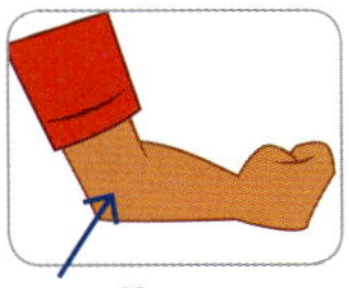
elbow

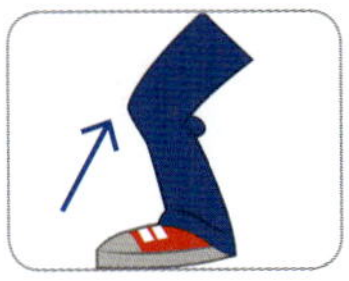
knee

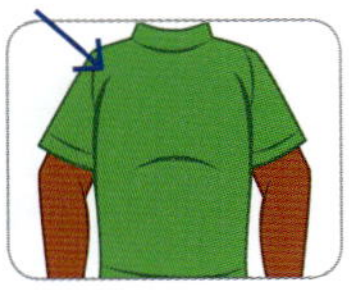
shoulder

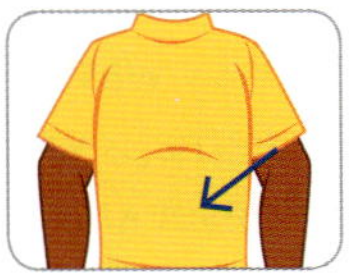
stomach

tail

throat

### 7 Match. Then name the other parts.

1 ankle ☐
2 elbow ☐
3 knee ☐
4 shoulder ☐
5 stomach ☐

### 8 Listen to the conversation. Tick all the facts that are true. TR: 6.4

☐ Regina broke her ankle.
☐ Regina hasn't ever fallen off a skateboard.
☐ Regina's ankle hurts.
☐ Regina broke her arm playing basketball.
☐ Regina has had a cold recently.
☐ Regina has finished playing basketball for the year.

### 9 Look at the picture and describe it using the present perfect simple and past simple. Use words from Activity 5.

### 10 Write a paragraph about the picture in Activity 9.

# Lesson 2

**1** **Listen. Listen and repeat.** TR: 6.5

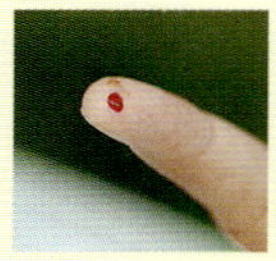
bleed

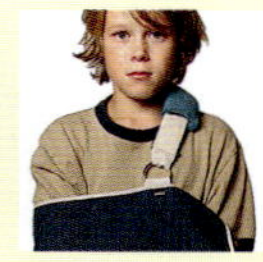
injure

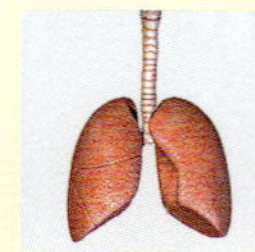
lungs

mummy

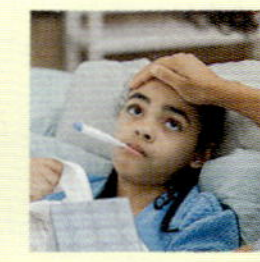
ill

weak

**2** **Listen and read.** TR: 6.6

arrowhead

## The Mystery of Ötzi the Iceman

In 1991, two hikers made an amazing discovery: a 5,300-year-old **mummy**. Called Ötzi, because he was found in the Ötzal Alps of Italy, this mummy was in ice for thousands of years. Because of this, scientists have been able to learn a lot from Ötzi's ancient body.

When he died, Ötzi was aged about 45, an old man. He was in poor health. His **lungs** were black and he had worm eggs inside his stomach, which probably made him **ill**. His bones were **weak**, especially in his shoulders, knees and ankles. Ötzi had 61 tattoos on his skin.

Studying Ötzi's body helps scientists understand life back then. Scientists found clothing and equipment that show Ötzi was an important man. Studies of his teeth tell scientists where he lived. They even learnt that Ötzi ate just two hours before he died.

What scientists cannot fully understand is Ötzi's death. After much testing, they learnt that somebody killed Ötzi. They found an arrowhead in his left shoulder that caused **bleeding**. He also had a head **injury**. Scientists have got a lot of information, but there are still questions: Why was Ötzi in the mountains? Why was he killed? Perhaps we'll never know.

**Guess what!** Scientists have also found 19 people who are descendants of Ötzi. In 2017, they were still living in the region of Austria near where his body was found.

**3** **Circle the correct words.**

1 Ötzi is a 5,300-year-old **mummy** / **hiker**.

2 Scientists can study Ötzi because he was kept in **clothes** / **ice**.

3 **Worms** / **Tattoos** made Ötzi ill.

4 Ötzi died from **the cold temperatures** / **bleeding and a head injury**.

5 We may never know **how Ötzi lived** / **why Ötzi was killed**.

**4** **Write the words from Activity 1 next to each definition.**

1 ______________ Not well

2 ______________ A body that has been kept for thousands of years

3 ______________ Part of the body that moves air in and out of your body

4 ______________ Not strong

5 ______________ To hurt someone or something

## GRAMMAR Possessive pronouns

We use possessive pronouns when something belongs to someone or when someone has a particular relationship with something.
*That necklace is **mine**!*

A possessive pronoun replaces a possessive adjective and a noun.
*That's her medicine. = It's **hers**.*

We can also use possessive pronouns with *so* to agree with someone.
*'My hands are cold.' 'So are **hers**.'*
*'My head hurts.' 'So does **mine**.'*

**Possessive adjectives**

my his her your our their

**Possessive pronouns**

mine his hers yours ours theirs

### 5 Listen. Listen and repeat. TR: 6.7

**ancient** Ötzi used ancient tools for hunting.
**mystery** A mystery is something that people can't understand.
**skin** Skin is the outside layer of your body.
**sore** After lots of exercise, your body can become sore.
**tattoo** In many cultures, people put tattoos on their bodies.

### 6 Match.

1 ancient a having aches
2 mystery b covers everyone's body
3 skin c body art
4 sore d unknown thing
5 tattoo e very old

### 7 Circle the correct words.

1 'Is that Mum's ring?' 'Yes, it's **her** / **hers**.'
2 Which sweatshirt is **yours** / **your**?
3 'Are these books **their** / **theirs**?'
4 That's **my** / **mine** face in the mirror.
5 Don't take that medicine. It isn't **our** / **ours**.

### 8 Replace the words in bold with the correct possessive pronoun.

1 Those photos are **grandad's**. ________
2 'Whose bag is this?' 'It's **Anna's**.' ________
3 Is that cat **your cat**? ________
4 Was this your idea or was it **their idea**? ________
5 We own this jewellery. It's **our jewellery**. ________

### 9 Listen. Tick the correct answer. TR: 6.8

1 Who does Mrs Myers call?
☐ a scientist
☐ a doctor
☐ Grandad

2 What's wrong with the twins?
☐ They've got a stomach ache.
☐ They've got a cold.
☐ They've got a temperature.

3 What's wrong with Grandad?
☐ He's sore.
☐ He's coughing.
☐ He's got sunburn.

4 What has Mrs Myers got?
☐ A sore throat
☐ A tattoo
☐ A headache

### SOUNDS OF ENGLISH TR: 6.9, 6.10

**A** Listen. How do we say the letters in red?
1 boy**s**, toy**s**, doe**s**, arm**s**, leg**s**, Jame**s**, Charle**s**
2 hurt**s**, **s**illy, **s**at, **s**ore, **s**ick, le**ss**on

**B** Listen and repeat the rhyme.

Charles and James are two silly boys.
They sat in the sun and played with their toys
For seven hours, maybe more
And now their faces are red and sore.
'My head hurts!' 'So does mine!'
'We feel sick and we're not fine.
Our arms and legs are very burnt.
What a lesson we have learnt.'

# Lesson 3

**1 Listen and read the tips for healthy living. Which of them do you already follow?** TR: 6.11

## Tips for Healthy Living

Kids don't often think about aches and pains. They just want to play and have fun, don't they? But even kids need to make sure they take good care of themselves. Follow these easy tips to have a healthy life.

- Stay active! Don't spend all your time in front of a screen. Your body gets weak if you don't use it. Play a sport, go running or simply go for a walk, but get outside.
- Be careful of what you put in your school bag! Too many books can give you backache. Try to take only two or three books home at a time. And leave anything you don't need at school. If your bag is still too heavy, ask a friend to help you carry something.
- Make sure you eat different types of healthy foods, including lots of fruit and vegetables. And drink lots of water to keep your body hydrated, especially when you're exercising or outside in the sun!
- When you do exercise, make sure you stretch. If body parts like your ankles, knees and wrists are weak, you can injure them easily. Regular stretching helps make these body parts strong.
- Get enough sleep. Try to sleep at least nine hours each night.
- Make sure you visit the doctor every year. Even if you don't feel ill, it's important that your doctor sees you. She might discover a problem that you didn't know about. You should also talk to your doctor about things like trying new sports.

**2 Answer the following questions.**

1 How does your body become weak?

2 Why is stretching important?

3 Why mustn't you carry more than two or three books in your school bag?

4 What do you think the word hydrated means?

5 How much sleep do you get every night? How does it compare with the reading?

6 What should you talk to your doctor about?

### SAY IT LIKE THIS!

**At the doctor's**

**Complete the dialogue with these phrases.**

I've got a bad cough. Is it serious?
Open your mouth. Take this medicine.
What's the matter?

**Doctor:** (1) ____________

**Patient:** (2) ____________ My throat's really sore, too.

**Doctor:** Let me see. (3) ____________ OK, that's fine.

**Patient:** (4) ____________

**Doctor:** No, it isn't. (5) ____________ You'll be fine in a few days.

## 3 Listen and complete the dialogue. TR: 6.12

**Lizzie:** What's wrong, Grandma? Are you OK?

**Grandma:** Well, I've got a pain in my (1) ____________________.

**Lizzie:** Oh, dear.

**Grandma:** And my (2) ____________________ is a bit sore again.

**Lizzie:** Yes, it's been sore for a while. What about your (3) ____________________? Have you taken your (4) ____________________?

**Grandma:** Yes, I took my medicine this morning. Grandpa took his medicine, too. He had a (5) ____________________.

**Lizzie:** Oh, dear. I hope he's OK.

**Grandma:** Yes. Don't worry. He's fine now!

## 4 Find four differences between the two pictures. Use have/has got and there is/are.

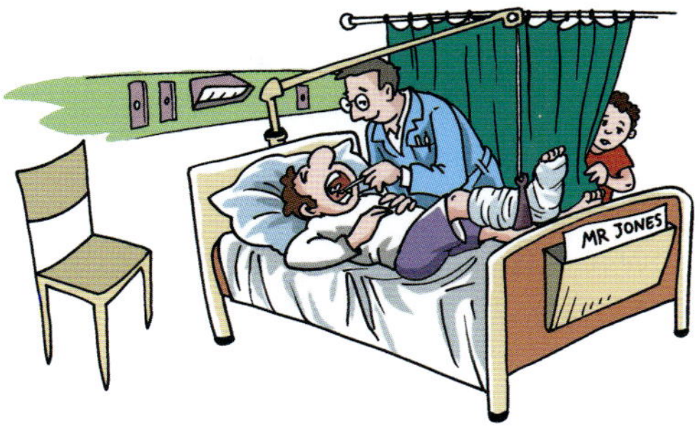


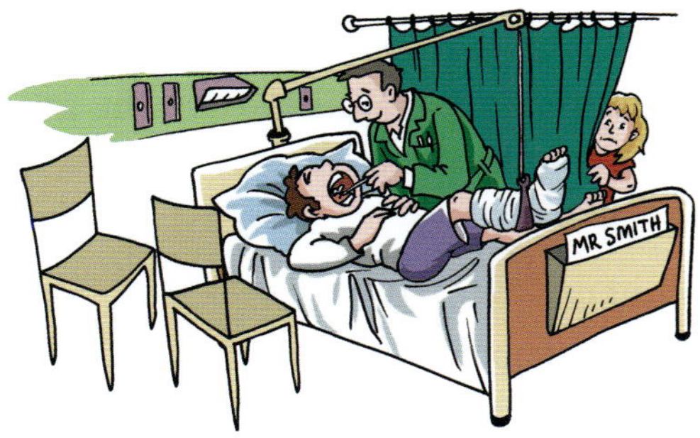


## WRITING Order of paragraphs

### A Read about the order of paragraphs in letters and emails.

A piece of writing has a beginning, a middle and an end. In the first paragraph of an email we introduce the subject. In the middle paragraph(s), we give more detail about the topic and in the final paragraph, we conclude our writing. We often ask about the person we are writing to in the final paragraph, too.

### B Now read the email below and number the paragraphs in the correct order.

**Email**

Hi Linda,

☐ After we ate, I took Tomo to the park. We met my friend Kim there. Do you remember her?

☐ Hi! How are you? I'm fine. I'm writing because I didn't call yesterday. I took my dog Tomo to the vet.

☐ Well, it's time for bed now. Write soon and let me know your news.

☐ Tomo has been sick all week. Usually, he plays a lot but this week he just sat on his bed. He didn't do anything and he wasn't hungry. The vet was really nice. She said 'Don't worry, he's just got a stomach ache. Give him this medicine and he'll be fine.' She was right. This morning, he was hungry again and he ate his breakfast.

See you soon!
Sarita

### C Write an email to a friend about when someone was sick. Use this plan to help you.

**Begin like this:**
Hi (name),

**Paragraph 1**
Write one or two sentences. Say why you are writing.

**Paragraphs 2 and 3**
Explain what has happened and give details.

**Paragraph 4**
Say goodbye to your friend and ask for his/her news.

**Finish like this:**
See you soon!

### D Read your email and check that it's got a beginning, a middle and an end.

# Review

## 1 Label the photos.

________

________

________

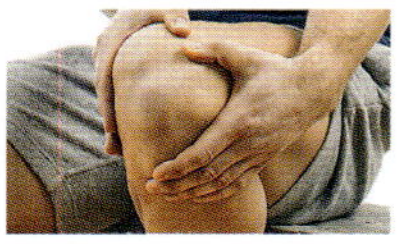
________

## 2 Complete the table.

boarding school chest cough head teacher shoulder sneeze temperature report throat

| Body | Education | Health |
|---|---|---|
| ________ | ________ | ________ |
| ________ | ________ | ________ |
| ________ | ________ | ________ |

## 3 Choose the correct answer.

1 If a virus enters your body, you can ____.

a catch a cold b injure your knee c bleed

2 A teacher with lots of rules is very ____.

a fair b strict c sick

3 When you've got a cold, you ____.

a hurt your ankle b have got a sore elbow c cough and sneeze

4 The ____ tells you that the lesson has finished.

a canteen b bell c test

5 Your ____ is not part of your leg.

a chest b ankle c knee

6 Ötzi is a(n) ____ mummy.

a weak b ancient c sore

## 4 Circle the correct answers.

1 I'm so hungry! I haven't eaten **for** / **since** hours!

2 We've been on holiday **for** / **since** the middle of July. I'm ready for school.

3 He's **never** / **ever** studied for a test, but he always gets high marks.

4 John isn't at school now. He's **already** / **for** left.

5 Have you **ever** / **never** had a bad report?

6 Have you finished your test **just** / **yet**?

## 5 Complete the sentences with the present perfect simple of the words in brackets.

1 Judy ________ (go) to the library to study for her history test.

2 ________ (you / see) a mummy?

3 James and I ________ (not finish) our project on ancient Egypt.

4 Jason ________ (read) the book twice.

5 How long ________ (you / have) that bad cough?

6 He ________ (not say) anything to us all day!

## 6 Complete the paragraph with the present perfect simple or past simple of the verbs in brackets.

My pet cat, Nico, (1) ________ (be) ill for three days now. I (2) ________ (have) Nico since we (3) ________ (move) here. We (4) ________ (go) to the vet this morning because I was a bit worried about her. She (5) ________ (not eat) since yesterday and she doesn't want to play. The vet (6) ________ (take) her temperature and gave me two kinds of medicine for her. She's got a sore throat but the vet says she'll be fine in a day or two.

## 7 Choose the correct answers.

1 'Hey, Zaida, is that your notebook?'
'No, it isn't ______.'

a mine    b yours

2 My throat is really sore. How's ______, Alexis?

a your    b yours

3 These classrooms all look the same. How do we know which one is ______?

a ours    b mine

4 This book is Mum's but the magazine isn't ______. It's Grandma's.

a his    b hers

5 We haven't got a canteen at our school but my brothers say is ______ brilliant.

a ours    b theirs

6 'Are those Grandpa's glasses on the table?'
'No, he's wearing ______, those are Mum's'.

a his    b him

## 8 Write sentences about yourself, using these words.

1 yesterday ______________________________

______________________________

2 already ______________________________

______________________________

3 yet ______________________________

______________________________

4 last month ______________________________

______________________________

5 never ______________________________

______________________________

## Song TR: 6.13

We've all got a head and shoulders
A stomach and knees and toes
Hands, arms, legs and fingers,
Mouth, teeth, eyes and nose.

With our feet, ears, throats and faces
We can walk, hear, cough and cry
Our bodies do what we want them to do.
We're amazing, you and I.

We must eat good food and exercise
We'll be healthy and strong
We must look after our bodies
And make good choices all day long!

# Video

## 1 BEFORE YOU WATCH

**What do you do at school? Tick.**

- ☐ read books and articles
- ☐ listen to my teacher during lessons
- ☐ wear a uniform
- ☐ do my homework
- ☐ write reports
- ☐ do exams

I ______________________ .

**Now talk about what you have never done at school.**

I have never arrived late.

I have never played on my phone.

## 2 WORDS TO KNOW

**Match the words to the pictures.**

pollinate | bee suit | honeycomb | beehive

______________

______________

______________

______________

## 3 WHILE YOU WATCH

**Circle the things that you can see in the video.**

| | |
|---|---|
| bee suits | students eating sandwiches |
| uniforms | flowers |
| exams | students taking time off from school |
| beehives | |

## 4 AFTER YOU WATCH

**Tick T for *True* or F for *False*.**

1 People who take care of bees are called beekeepers. T F

2 Beekeepers wear bee suits. T F

3 Bees make the sound 'bump bump bump'. T F

4 Bees help to produce the food we eat. T F

5 The students in the video are too scared of bees to learn about them. T F

## 5 WATCH AGAIN.

**What do you know about bees? Talk about it.**

I know that bees make honey.

Yes! And they pollinate flowers!

# 7

# All Around Us

Ice climbing at Athabasca Glacier during the aurora borealis, Canada

**1** **Look at the photo. Answer the questions.**

1 What colours can you see?
2 What time of day is it?
3 What is the person doing?

# Lesson 1

**1 Listen. Listen and repeat.** TR: 7.1

iguana

jungle

sand

volcano

wildlife

erupt
national park

**2 Listen and read.** TR: 7.2

Rosa: Bruno, I'm so excited. We're going to visit Costa Rica this summer.

Bruno: Cool! Where are you going in Costa Rica?

Rosa: We're going to explore a huge **national park**, Parque Tortuguero.

Bruno: How long will you be there?

Rosa: We're going to spend four days there.

Bruno: What are you going to do there?

Rosa: Well, there's a **jungle**, a **volcano** and a beach. We'll explore all three.

Bruno: How are you going to explore the jungle?

Rosa: Well, on the first day, we'll walk through the jungle. I'm going to take lots of photos. There's amazing **wildlife**, like the red-eyed tree frog and the green **iguana**. It's going to be awesome!

Bruno: And on the second day?

Rosa: We're going on a boat tour through the jungle. I'm sure we'll see monkeys and crocodiles – they're everywhere. On the third day, we'll explore the area near the Arenal Volcano. It's one of the most active volcanoes on Earth!

Bruno: Really? Will you be safe?

Rosa: Of course. They're not going to take us if it's **erupting**.

Bruno: I hope not! And what will you do on the fourth day?

Rosa: This is the day I'm most excited about. We're going to visit the beach to see where the turtles lay their eggs. We're going to see some baby turtles in the **sand**.

Bruno: Sounds great, Rosa!

**3 Write the word. Then match.**

1 s ___ ___ ___

2 ___ ___ u ___ ___ ___

3 ___ ___ ___ g ___ ___

4 ___ ___ ___ ___ l ___ ___ ___

5 ___ ___ ___ a ___ ___

**a** A type of large lizard that lives in Central and South America

**b** What's on the ground at the beach

**c** A tropical forest with lots of plants and wildlife

**d** What an active volcano does

**e** Animals that live in nature

**4 Read and complete the sentences with information from the text.**

1 Rosa is going to spend four days at a __________ in Costa Rica.

2 On the first day, Rosa is going to see wildlife such as __________ and __________.

3 On the second day, she'll explore the __________ by boat.

4 On the third day, Rosa will visit a __________, if it's not __________.

5 Finally, Rosa will go to the beach. She wants to see baby turtles in the __________.

## 5 Listen. Listen and repeat. TR: 7.3

branch

lay eggs

leaf

nest

soil

stone

## 6 Complete the sentences with these words.

| branch | lay eggs | leaves | nest |
|---|---|---|---|
| soil | stones | | |

1 Sea turtles ________________ on the beach.

2 The bird made a ________________ for her eggs.

3 In autumn, the ________________ change colour.

4 There's no sand on this beach, only little ________________.

5 This ________________ is good for farming.

6 Look at the beautiful bird on that tree ________________.

### GRAMMAR Future simple

We use the future simple:

**a** for predictions about the future.
*It **will rain** all day tomorrow.*

**b** for decisions that we make now.
*I'**ll look after** the plants.*

**c** for offers, promises and warnings.
*Don't touch that dog, it **will bite** you.*

**d** to ask someone for help.
***Will** you **feed** the birds, please?*

**e** after **think** and **be sure**:
*I'**m sure** the soil **will be** wet.*

### GRAMMAR Be going to

We use **be going to**:

**a** to talk about future plans and intentions.
*I'**m going to be** in Costa Rica in June.*

**b** to predict that something will happen when we have some proof or information.
*It'**s going to rain** later. They said so on TV.*

## 7 Complete the sentences with the correct form of the future simple or be going to and the verbs in brackets.

1 Don't worry. I saw on my phone that it ________________ (not rain).

2 I'm sure it ________________ (be) hot in the jungle.

3 You look tired, Mum. I ________________ (cook) dinner.

4 ________________ (you / take) my turtle to the vet, please?

5 ________________ (he / come) with us? Has he decided yet?

## 8 Listen. Change the words in bold to make the sentences true. TR: 7.4

1 It's going to **snow**. ________________

2 They will not go to the **zoo**. ________________

3 They will have lunch at **school**. ________________

4 Sam has got **four** sandwiches. He **will** be hungry. ________________

5 They'll leave the school at **ten** o'clock. ________________

## 9 Imagine that you are going to the zoo tomorrow. Ask and answer these questions with your partner.

1 What are you going to see there?

2 What do you think will happen?

## 10 Write a paragraph about your trip to the zoo tomorrow. Use the future simple and be going to.

# Lesson 2

**1** **Listen. Listen and repeat.** TR: 7.5

creature

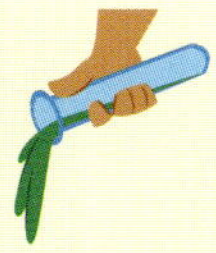

liquid

stem

trap

humid
smell

**2** **Listen and read.** TR: 7.6

What do plants need to grow? If you said light, soil and water, you're right! But some plants have got different needs – they eat meat! Meat-eating plants usually grow in areas with poor soil. This soil can't give them enough food, so they've found another way to get it: eating insects and other small **creatures**. (Don't worry, though. Plants only eat people in books and films!)

One well-known meat-eating plant is the Venus flytrap. It grows in very **humid** climates with lots of insects. Insects fly into the plant because it's got a bright, red colour and a fruity **smell**. When the insect lands, the leaves close together and **trap** it inside.

Another meat-eating plant is the pitcher plant. There are several varieties of pitcher plant, and some of them can become very big, with stems up to 6 m. (20 ft.) long, and flowers 1 m. (3.3 ft.) high. They can hold up to two litres of sweet, sticky **liquid**. Curious animals go inside for a drink, but then they slide down the plant's slippery side and become its next meal. And it's not always thirsty insects that go into pitcher plants. Finding a mouse or a lizard inside a pitcher plant is not too unusual.

These beautiful plants attract animals with their sweet smells, and then they eat them. Who knew that plants could be so clever?

**Guess what!** Scientists have learned that Venus flytraps don't kill insects immediately. They respond to an insect's movement. An insect that is trapped but doesn't move might be able to leave the plant alive when the trap opens again.

**3** **Answer the questions.**

1 Where do a lot of meat-eating plants grow?
2 Why do these plants 'eat' meat?
3 Which plant traps insects inside its leaves?
4 Why do animals go into pitcher plants?
5 How big can some pitcher plants get?
6 How much liquid can a pitcher plant hold?

**4** **Complete the sentences with words from Activity 1.**

1 It's very ________________. It's going to rain.
2 Milk is a type of ________________.
3 A plant's got leaves and a ________________.
4 A hunter will ________________ animals.
5 I love the ________________ of hot coffee.
6 What is that ________________ in the garden?

## 5 Listen. Listen and repeat. TR: 7.7

**alive** Eating insects keeps a Venus flytrap alive.

**curious** Monkeys are very curious animals. They want to explore everything!

**massive** Some meat-eating plants have massive flowers that are one metre high.

**slippery** The water on the floor made it very slippery.

**sticky** Insects can't move on the sticky leaves of a Venus flytrap.

## 6 Circle the correct words.

1 The mouse is lucky it's **alive** / **curious** after falling into a pitcher plant.

2 Look at that strange plant. Aren't you **slippery** / **curious** about it?

3 There was a **massive** / **sticky** bear outside the window. It was so big!

4 My hands are very **curious** / **sticky** after touching this liquid.

5 Animals slide into pitcher plants because their sides are **slippery** / **alive**.

### GRAMMAR Gerunds

Gerunds are nouns which we make from verbs. We add **–ing** to the verb to form them.
We can use gerunds:

**a** as the subject of a sentence.
*__Playing__ with snakes can be dangerous.*

**b** as the object of a sentence.
*I like __running__ in the fields.*

**c** after prepositions.
*I'm not very good at __looking__ after plants.*

**d** after verbs such as **can't stand**, **dislike**, **like**, **love**, **enjoy**, **miss**, **hate** and **remember**.
*I __enjoy feeding__ the squirrels.*

## 7 Look back at the article. Underline the gerunds. How many are there?

## 8 Complete the sentences with gerunds.

catch feed stay swim watch

1 Don't think about ______________ TV this afternoon. We're working in the garden.

2 My cat likes ______________ mice.

3 ______________ in the sea is great fun.

4 I enjoy ______________ the birds on the balcony. I give them birdseed.

5 The dogs can't stand ______________ in the garden. They like going out.

## 9 Listen. Complete the sentences. TR: 7.8

1 Brian likes watching TV and ______________ with his dog.

2 Alisa thinks ______________ is a waste of time.

3 Alisa loves watching birds and ______________.

4 David thinks ______________ is boring.

5 David enjoys ______________ the zoo.

## 10 With a partner, discuss the following.

1 What's a smell you really like? Dislike?

2 What are you most curious about?

3 What activity in nature do you most enjoy?

## 11 Complete these sentences with gerunds. Then share your responses with a partner.

1 I like ______________.

2 I hate ______________.

3 I miss ______________.

4 I remember ______________ when I was a child.

### SOUNDS OF ENGLISH TR: 7.9, 7.10

**A** Listen and repeat the words. Which words rhyme?

bought rough thought dough
brought though tough

**B** Listen. Repeat the tongue twister.

I brought the tough dough you bought.
Though I thought you brought the
rough dough I bought.

# Lesson 3

**1** **Listen and read about the threats facing turtles and what's being done. What can you do to help turtles?** TR: 7.11

## Let's Take Care of Our Turtles!

Turtles are amazing creatures, aren't they? Turtles have been on Earth for millions of years, but now nearly 70 per cent of turtle species are endangered.

Some of the reasons that turtles are endangered include:

- People want to have turtles as pets, but they're not surviving and having babies like they do in the wild.
- More and more people are eating turtle meat, which causes population loss.
- Turtles get caught in fishing nets by accident and are dying.
- Hungry turtles are eating plastic that's in the ocean, which is making them sick.

14

Around the world, people have opened turtle sanctuaries – protected areas that help turtles stay alive and protect their eggs. One example is in Bora Bora. In 1991, a tourist at the Hotel Le Méridien brought an injured turtle to the hotel. After that, the hotel opened a turtle protection centre. It works to help turtles protect their babies, treat injured turtles and teach hotel visitors about the danger turtles are in. The sanctuary is a success, and it's growing. Visitors are returning home and sharing the message about endangered turtles. And this is just one example. By sharing information and helping turtles, we can make a difference, can't we?

**2** **Circle the correct answers.**

1 Seventy per cent of turtle species are **pets** / **endangered**.

2 Turtles accidentally die when **hunters get them for food** / **they get caught in fishing nets**.

3 Turtles are getting sick eating **eggs** / **plastic**.

4 The turtle protection centre opened in Bora Bora after a **turtle ate a plastic bag** / **tourist brought an injured turtle into the hotel**.

5 The centre wants to **teach guests about** / **hide from guests** the dangers turtles are in.

### SAY IT LIKE THIS!

**Talking about animals.**

This animal is hairy/furry/cute/smooth/slimy/friendly/funny/cuddly/jumpy.

It likes sleeping/eating/running/jumping/climbing/playing catch/doing tricks.

*Look at the frog. It's slimy and jumpy.*
*It likes jumping and hiding.*

*My pet is a rabbit. It's furry and cute.*
*It likes eating carrots and sleeping.*

**Talk to your partner about a pet or any animal you know. Practise the language above.**

## GRAMMAR Question tags

We use question tags:

**a** to confirm our opinion.
*This forest is amazing, **isn't it**?*

**b** when we are pretty sure that what we say is true.
*You've got a big garden, **haven't you**?*

We make question tags with an auxiliary verb and a subject pronoun. We use the auxiliary verb that we use for the tense in the main part of the sentence.
*Those dogs aren't running, **are they**?*

For affirmative sentences in the present simple we use **do/does** and for sentences in the past simple we use **did**.
*They didn't go to see the turtles, **did they**?*

When the sentence uses a verb in the affirmative, we use a negative question tag. When the sentence uses a verb in the negative, we use an affirmative question tag.
*We go to the park often, **don't we**?*
*He hasn't been to Bora Bora this year, **has he**?*

We can use questions tags in all tenses and with modal verbs.
*Elephants can swim, **can't they**?*

**3 Match.**

1 That animal isn't yours,
2 We want a quiet dog,
3 The boys haven't got a pet yet,
4 He doesn't like animals much,
5 Your rabbit did tricks,

a have they?
b didn't it?
c is it?
d does he?
e don't we?

**4 Complete the sentences with question tags.**

1 You are going to eat that, ____________?
2 We worked hard all day, ____________?
3 That animal's dangerous, ____________?
4 She hasn't cleaned yet, ____________?
5 You can see the birds, ____________?

## WRITING Punctuation

**A Look at these punctuation rules.**

Sentences begin with a capital letter and end with a full stop or a question mark:
*The rabbits ate all the carrots in the garden.*
*Does James like gardening?*

Names of people and places start with a capital letter:
*Ahmed and Ismael are going to Cairo.*

We use an exclamation mark for emphasis:
*What a beautiful animal!*

We use commas to separate words in a list and to separate question tags from the rest of the sentence:
*Pets need love, exercise, fun and healthy food.*
*It's cold today, isn't it?*

**B Add the T, t or a correct punctuation mark.**

1 Is this your farm ____
2 ____ hat rabbit is cute!
3 I like frogs ____ turtles and iguanas.
4 What a big nest ____

**C Miguel wrote too fast! Correct his postcard's punctuation and capitalisation.**

Hi tom,

how are you thanks for the photos of your holiday what a great beach you went to

i'm writing this from my holiday home yesterday I found a cat in the street we're going to find his owner and take him back to his home his name is rocco

i've taken a picture of rocco he's great isn't he you can see he's got green eyes and large ears don't you love him

see you soon

miguel

**D Write a message to a friend about an animal you saw. Use this plan to help you.**

**Paragraph 1:** Ask about your friend.

**Paragraph 2:** Say where you are writing from. Talk about the animal you saw.

**Paragraph 3:** Talk about the picture of the animal. Describe the animal and the place you saw it.

**Ending:** See you soon!

**E Read your message and check the punctuation and capital letters.**

# 8 Protecting the Planet

Sunset on a winter's evening on Glass Beach, California

**1 Look at the photo. Answer the questions.**

1 What do you think is on the beach?

2 What can you do to protect the planet?

# Lesson 1

**1** **Listen. Listen and repeat.** TR: 8.1

cover

dump

landfill

environmental
improve
system

**2** **Listen and read.** TR: 8.2

## Sai Tso Wan Recreation Centre: From Landfill to Lovely

### How one landfill in Hong Kong became a popular park

The Sai Tso Wan Recreation Centre shows that if we work to **improve** our environment, we will make a difference in people's lives!

**Then (Before 1995)**

- This land was the Sai Tso Wan **Landfill**.
- Hong Kong **dumped** 1.6 million tonnes of rubbish here.
- This rubbish took up two hectares (five acres) of land.
- This area used to smell really bad!

**What changed (1995-2004)**

- Workers **covered** the rubbish with clean soil.
- They checked to see if the land was safe to use.
- They made sure the park's energy came from the sun and wind.
- They created a **system** to collect rainwater for the park.

**Now (2004-present)**

- There is a huge playground with a rubber floor.
- There is a jogging track.
- There are fields for football and baseball. In fact, the park is the official training site for the Hong Kong Baseball Association, the national baseball team.
- There's an **environmental** centre to teach visitors about how Hong Kong handles rubbish.

**3** **Unscramble. Then match.**

1 msyets ____________
2 pioremv ____________
3 ocerv ____________
4 pmdu ____________
5 falnidll ____________

a Throw away something you don't need
b Way of doing something
c A place for people's rubbish
d Make better
e Put something over another thing

**4** **Read. Write B for Before, C for Change, or N for Now.**

1 People dump rubbish onto this area. ☐
2 Workers check to make sure the land was safe. ☐
3 The Hong Kong Baseball Association trains on this site. ☐
4 Workers use green energy and rainwater in their plans. ☐
5 This area smells really bad. ☐
6 Children can play in the playground. ☐

## GRAMMAR First conditional

We use the first conditional to talk about something which will probably happen in the present or in the future. Sentences in the first conditional have two clauses. The *if* clause uses *if* followed by the present simple, and the result clause uses the future simple.

***If we recycle** batteries, **we will help** the environment.*

In the first conditional, one or both of the clauses can be negative.

*If you **don't recycle**, we **will have** a lot of rubbish!*
*If we **don't look after** our beaches, they **won't be** clean.*

We can ask questions with first conditional sentences with and without question words:
*What will happen if we destroy the environment?*
*Will this rubbish smell bad if we leave it here?*

**Note:** It doesn't matter which clause comes first, but if we put the *if* clause first then we use a comma. If the result clause comes first, we don't use a comma.

*If you grow flowers, your garden will be beautiful.*

*Your garden will be beautiful if you grow flowers.*

**5 Listen. Listen and repeat.** TR: 8.3

battery

can

cardboard

electronics

newspaper

plastic bag

**6 Complete the sentences with words from Activity 5.**

1 This shop sells smartphones, tablets and other ______.
2 The new ______ I bought are too big for my video game. I need smaller ones.
3 Grandpa likes reading the ______.
4 My mum always takes her own bags to the shop so she doesn't use ______.
5 Jon put everything on his desk into a ______ box, and then took it home.

**7 Circle the correct words.**

1 If you **collect** / **will collect** cans and bottles at school, I will put them in the bins.
2 Will we help the environment if we **don't use** / **won't use** a lot of water?
3 You will see some pictures of animals if you **won't turn on** / **turn on** the camera.
4 Plants **won't die** / **die** if you water them.

**8 Complete the first conditional sentences with the verbs in brackets.**

1 If she ______ (go) for a walk, she will pick up any litter she sees.
2 The park ______ (not be) nice if they don't clean it.
3 They will collect all your rubbish if you ______ (leave) it outside.
4 ______ (you / help) me tidy the garden if I pay you?
5 If they clean the beaches near here this summer, I ______ (swim) in the sea.

**9 Listen. Complete the sentences.** TR: 8.4

1 The class is going to learn about ______.
2 Elsa's parents recycle paper, glass and ______.
3 Manos's mum recycles old ______.
4 Manos's dad takes some things to a special ______ in the town centre.
5 Students can recycle things at school in the big green ______.

**10 Discuss these questions with a partner.**

1 Do you think recycling is important? Why?
2 What do you recycle at home? How often?

**11 Write a paragraph about recycling. Answer the questions from Activity 10.**

# Lesson 2

**1** **Listen. Listen and repeat.** TR: 8.5

|  |  |  |  |  |  |  |
|---|---|---|---|---|---|---|
| destroy | oil | petrol | pollute | recycle | tap water | throw away |

**2** **Listen and read.** TR: 8.6

## Go Green: Drink a Glass of Water

Why do people drink water from plastic bottles? Some think it's cleaner than **tap water**. Others think it's easier to carry. But do you know the effects of buying water in plastic bottles? Once you do, you may never buy it again!

- First, we need a lot of **oil** to make plastic products. Oil is a source of energy, and we depend on it for lots of things. In fact, if we used the oil for a year's worth of water bottles to make **petrol** instead, we would fill 1 million cars for a year.
- Second, plastic bottles **pollute** the environment. If we **recycled** all our plastic bottles, there would be less rubbish in landfills. But people still **throw away** lots of plastic, and much of it goes into the sea: over 5 million tonnes each year. This plastic is **destroying** the ocean's ecosystem by making seabirds and animals sick.
- Third, look at the price. Tap water is almost free, but bottled water costs money – lots more money than tap water. And some bottled water is just tap water sold in a bottle! In fact, one report shows that 47 per cent of bottled water is from the tap. That's almost half!

So, the next time you feel thirsty, stop and think. Do you buy a bottle of water? Or do you get a glass of tap water? Your actions make a difference.

**Guess what!** Seabirds often eat plastic from the ocean by mistake. To them, the plastic looks like, and even smells like, food!

**3** **Read and tick T for *True* or F for *False*.**

1 People use plastic products to make oil, such as petrol. T F

2 People recycle all the plastic water bottles they use. T F

3 Five million tonnes of plastic goes into the sea each year. T F

4 Most bottled water is free. T F

5 Almost half of the bottled water sold is really tap water. T F

**4** **Write the missing letters.**

1 To litter and throw rubbish in the sea

_ _ _ _ _ _ _

2 What comes from the tap

_ _ _  _ _ _ _ _

3 What most cars need

_ _ _ _ _ _

4 To badly break or hurt something

_ _ _ _ _ _ _

5 To put rubbish into the bin

_ _ _ _ _  _ _ _ _

## GRAMMAR Second conditional

We use the second conditional:

**a** to talk about something that cannot happen in the present or the future.
*If I had a garden, I'd be very happy!*

**b** to talk about something that is unlikely to happen in the present or the future.
*That plant would die if you watered it twice a day.*

**c** to give advice.
*If I were you, I'd start recycling.*

Sentences in the second conditional have two clauses. The *if* clause uses *if* followed by the past simple and the result clause uses **would** followed by a bare infinitive.
*I wouldn't destroy that if I were you.*

In the second conditional, one or both of the clauses can be negative.
*The city would be very dirty if we didn't recycle.*
*If we didn't keep our beaches clean, they wouldn't be nice.*

We can ask questions with second conditional sentences with and without question words:
*What would happen to the animals if there was a fire in the forest?*
*Would they throw away plastic bottles if they didn't see a bin?*

**Note:** We usually use **were** instead of **was** after the first and third person singular.

**5 Complete the second conditional sentences with the verbs in brackets.**

1 If she ______ (have) a plastic bottle, she ______ (use) it again.

2 ______ we ______ (help) the environment if we ______ (save) energy?

3 We ______ (not have) so much rubbish if we ______ (recycle) more.

4 If I ______ (be) you, I ______ (read) that article about the environment.

**6 Listen. Listen and repeat.** TR: 8.7

| | |
|---|---|
| **air conditioning** | On a hot day, many people use air conditioning. |
| **fan** | A fan blows air in a room. |
| **free** | Tap water doesn't cost anything: it's free. |
| **green** | One way to be green is to buy reusable bottles. |
| **product** | We must use fewer plastic products. |
| **waste** | A lot of food waste goes into landfills. |

**7 Circle the correct words.**

1 **A fan / Air conditioning** is a way to keep cool that uses little energy.

2 Many of the food **products / fans** we use come in plastic.

3 How much is that water bottle? It's **free / green**.

4 Putting the **air conditioning / waste** on every day uses a lot of energy.

5 I've got my reusable bag and bottle because I'm trying to be **free / green**.

6 Too much plastic **waste / fan** is going into the sea.

**8 Do the quiz. Listen and check.** TR: 8.8

1 How much rubbish from a litter bin can we recycle?
**a** 30% **b** 60% **c** 90%

2 Where can you recycle batteries?
**a** in green bins b in blue bins
**c** in supermarkets

3 How much of the waste in litter bins is plastic?
**a** 2% **b** 20% **c** 50%

4 Plastic bags pollute the environment for
**a** a minute. **b** a year. **c** 400 years.

### SOUNDS OF ENGLISH TR: 8.9, 8.10

**A** Listen and underline the stressed words.
If we really cared about the environment, we wouldn't have so many problems with pollution.

**B** Listen again. Circle the stressed words. How does the meaning of the sentence change the second time?

# Lesson 3

**1** **Listen and read the comments about the environment. What can you add to these ideas?** TR: 8.11

GO GREEN

HOME FEATURES BLOG CONTACT

**Enrique, 13, Galápagos Islands**

I live on a beautiful island. A lot of tourists come here every year and they throw away a lot of rubbish. My friends and I tell people, 'Never throw rubbish in the street or on the beach, always use a recycling bin or a litter bin.' We often clean the beach near our village and throw away the rubbish. There are so many amazing creatures living on our island! We must protect them from pollution.

**Sofia, 12, Lisbon**

If you plant a tree near your house, the shade will keep your home cool in the summer. Then, after the leaves fall in the autumn, the sun will heat your house. Trees are also good because they make oxygen. We breathe in oxygen so we can't live without it! Another thing you can do is use a fan instead of air conditioning because it saves energy.

**Carlos, 11, Madrid**

Do you eat snacks and then throw away your dinner? That is a waste! We throw away a lot of food every year. Making that food uses a lot of energy! Another way to go green is to use your bike or walk instead of using a car. Going green is easy!

**Amina, 12, Dubai**

Don't waste things! If a tap drips, you will waste a lot of water. One drop of water each second is over 10,000 litres of water a year! Also, find a recycling centre near you and recycle everything you can. And remember that you can use things again. You can use the same plastic bags many times before you recycle them, for example.

**2** **Write E for Enrique, S for Sofia, C for Carlos or A for Amina. Who …**

1 mentions the things we eat? ☐
2 talks about using things more than once? ☐
3 talks about transport? ☐
4 mentions seasons? ☐
5 collects rubbish? ☐

**SAY IT LIKE THIS!**

**Talking about the environment**

**Complete the dialogue with these words.**

pollute recycle ride throw away waste

**Kyra:** What do you do for the environment?
**Helen:** I (1) ________ cans, paper and bottles. What about you?
**Kyra:** I always (2) ________ my bike.
**Helen:** Do you (3) ________ food?
**Kyra:** I'm afraid I do, sometimes, but I never (4) ________. I always (5) ________ my rubbish in a bin.

**Practise the dialogue with your partner.**

**3 Listen and number the pictures in the correct order.** TR: 8.12

☐ 

☐ 

☐ 

☐ 

☐ 

**4 Look at the picture and say what you would do if you lived in this place.**

## WRITING Giving advice with conditionals

**A Look at these tips about the environment.**

1 Send emails instead of letters. You don't waste paper.

2 Turn off the light every time you leave a room. You save energy.

3 Recycle things. You help the environment.

**B Now complete the sentences in the second conditional using the tips from Activity A.**

1 If you ______________ instead of letters, you ______________ paper.

2 If you ______________ the light every time you left the room, you ______________ energy.

3 If you ______________, you ______________ the environment.

**C Look at the poster about the environment and complete the sentences using the second conditional.**

### POLLUTION

Don't pollute the environment! If we

(1) ______________ (throw) all our rubbish in bins, our city (2) ______________ (be) clean!

Take the bus or walk! If we (3) ______________ (stop) using cars all the time, we (4) ______________ (not pollute) the environment so much.

### RECYCLING

Recycle paper! We (5) ______________ (save) lots of trees if we (6) ______________ (recycle) all our paper.

### FOOD

Don't waste food. If we (7) ______________ (buy) only what we need, we (8) ______________ (not waste) anything.

**D Make a poster about the environment. Use this plan to help you and add photos or drawings to make the poster attractive.**

**Answer the questions for each part of the poster.**

What heading are you going to use?

What advice are you going to give under the heading?

What would happen if we followed the advice?

**E Remember to use the second conditional for the advice on your poster.**

# Review

## 1 Label the photos.

______

______

______

______

______

______

## 2 Match. Then write the word(s) on the line.

| | |
|---|---|
| 1 wild | **a** water ______ |
| 2 national | **b** bag ______ |
| 3 land | **c** fill ______ |
| 4 card | **d** park ______ |
| 5 plastic | **e** paper ______ |
| 6 news | **f** away ______ |
| 7 tap | **g** life ______ |
| 8 throw | **h** board ______ |

## 3 Circle the correct words.

1 A hot **liquid** / **sand** came from the volcano when it erupted.

2 The **stem** / **can** is the part of the plant that carries water.

3 Be careful. The wet floor is **sticky** / **slippery**.

4 That shop sells only green **products** / **cans**.

5 The **leaves** / **soil** must be wet before you start planting.

6 There is a horrible **smell** / **system** coming from the fridge.

7 She was **alive** / **curious** about the little creature on the beach.

## 4 Circle the correct words.

To take care of our planet, we must all **destroy** / **improve** our behaviour and make a difference. There are many little things we can do. First, we should visit a **national park** / **landfill**. If we enjoy nature, we will learn to care about environmental problems. Also, we create too much **petrol** / **waste**. Sixty per cent of what we **throw away** / **erupt** is recyclable, so we must pay attention because it matters. In fact, if we **pollute** / **recycle** a tonne of paper, we will save 17 trees and a lot of energy! We can buy a reusable bottle and fill it with **plastic** / **tap water** again and again. We must stop **smelling** / **destroying** our planet! Let's go green!

## 5 Complete the sentences with gerunds formed from the verbs in brackets.

1 I like ______ (learn) about environmental issues at school.

2 ______ (take) care of animals can be difficult.

3 I don't remember ______ (feed) the birds yesterday.

4 When it's winter, I miss ______ (sit) in Grandma's garden.

## 6 Choose the correct answers.

1 ____ water my plants next week, please?

**a** Are you going to **b** Will you

2 It ____ tomorrow. I saw it on the news.

**a** isn't snowing **b** isn't going to snow

3 Come on! ____ you plant those trees and bushes in the garden.

**a** I'll help **b** I'm going to help

4 Darren ____ put air conditioning in his bedroom. He told me yesterday.

**a** isn't going to **b** won't

**7** **Complete the sentences with question tags.**

1 You did turn off the tap, ____________ ?

2 The iguanas are in the sand, ____________ ?

3 That oil isn't hot, ____________ ?

4 She'll be OK in the jungle, ____________ ?

5 We can drink this water, ____________ ?

6 We don't need the fan today, ____________ ?

**8** **Complete the sentences with the correct form of the verbs in brackets. Use the first and the second conditional.**

1 If we ____________ (not look after) our environment, we will destroy it.

2 She ____________ (hurt) her sister if she's not careful.

3 If you grew your own food you ____________ (save) money.

4 You ____________ (use) less energy if you turn off the lights when you leave a room.

5 I'm afraid this torch won't work if you ____________ (not put) new batteries in it.

6 If I were you, I ____________ (ride) my bike to school every day.

**9** **Write two pieces of advice for taking care of the environment. Use the second conditional.**

______________________________________

______________________________________

______________________________________

______________________________________

## Song TR: 8.13

Dump rubbish everywhere
And we'll live in a dirty world.
Everyone can do something:
Every man, woman, boy and girl.

If we all recycled.
We would live in a world that's clean.
Fires destroy forests.
Planting trees will make the hills green.

We must protect the environment
And care for animals, too.
If we don't protect the environment,
What will our children do?

Think of life without animals,
Without wildlife in the sea:
There won't be any air for us
If we cut down every tree.

Yes, our climate's changing.
We must change, too, you and me.
If we were all more careful,
What a beautiful world this would be.

# Video

1 **BEFORE YOU WATCH**

**Where do you go when you go out in nature? Tick.**

- ☐ a national park
- ☐ a jungle
- ☐ a farm
- ☐ a volcano
- ☐ a beach

I _______________________________.

**Now talk about what you do in nature.**

2 **WORDS TO KNOW**

**Match the words to the pictures.**

global warming explorer tools generation

## 3 WHILE YOU WATCH

**What activities can you see the children doing in the video? Circle.**

watering plants
playing with cats and dogs
learning about the environment
planting seeds
playing with balls
riding bicycles

## 4 AFTER YOU WATCH

**Tick T for *True* or F for *False*.**

1 Maritza Morales Casanova teaches children about the environment and global warming. T F
2 Students also teach each other at the park. T F
3 Because students learn at the park, it isn't fun. T F
4 Maritza thinks it's important to take care of the environment. T F
5 Students only learn about plants. T F

## 5 WATCH AGAIN

**How are you going to teach others to care for the environment?**

I am going to teach my brother to turn off the tap when he brushes his teeth.

Cool! I am going to ask my dad to recycle old newspapers.

# 9 City Life

**1 Look at the photo and answer the questions.**

1 What are two ways people are getting around in this photo?

2 How can you describe this street scene?

A tram in Istanbul, Turkey

# Lesson 1

**design** **information** **sight** **location**
**follow (the) directions**

**1** **Listen. Listen and repeat.** TR: 9.1

**2** **Listen and read.** TR: 9.2

## Treasure Find
### City Scavenger Hunt

**What is Treasure Find?**

In a *Treasure Find* activity, you look for treasure in a city. We **design** each *Treasure Find* activity to help you explore a city and to learn about its most famous **sights**.

Treasure Find

START

**Name:** *The Bear and The Berry Tree*
**Location:** Puerta del Sol, Madrid town centre
**Date:** 1967
**Size:** 4 m (13 ft.) tall

**How does it work?**

First, find a team of 3 – 4 people. It's better to explore in a group. You must download the *Treasure Find* app. The phone will know your **location**. Touch 'Start' to begin your adventure. The app then gives you directions to your first place. **Follow** the **directions** to the first place. They're usually important buildings, statues or public parks.

Once you arrive, you'll get **information** about the place. You will have 30 seconds to study the information, and then you'll get a test. If you pass the test, you get easy directions to the next place. If not, the directions can be very difficult.

**How do we win?**

To win, your team has to go from place to place quickly. Once you get to the last place, there is a *Treasure Find* sign. Stand next to it and take a photo. Send your photo through the *Treasure Find* app. The app marks your time. Then, the *Treasure Find* team sends a message to the winner for each city. The winner each month gets a great prize!

**What are you waiting for? Start your adventure today!**

**3** **Write the words from Activity 1.**

1 _______________ A place
2 _______________ To go where signs or instructions tell you
3 _______________ To decide how something will look or work
4 _______________ What people know about something
5 _______________ Something tourists go to see

**4** **Answer the questions.**

1 How many people do you have to have for a team?
2 What do you have to do to begin your adventure?
3 How do you know where to go?
4 If you do badly on a test, what happens?
5 Who gets a prize?

**5** **Listen. Listen and repeat.** TR: 9.3

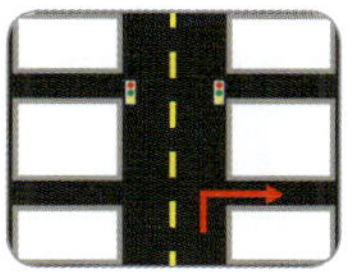

go around the corner

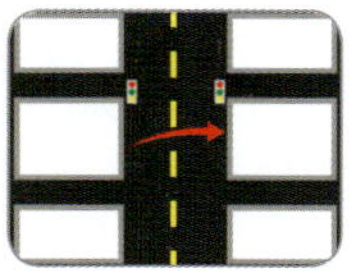

cross the road

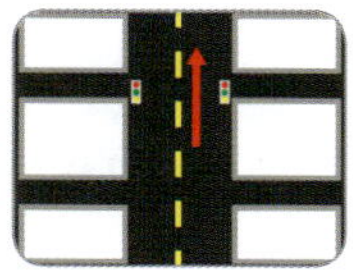

go past (the traffic lights)

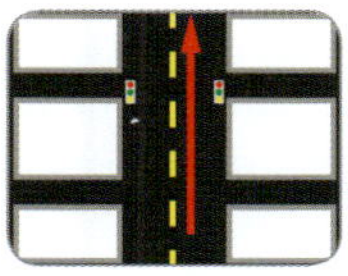

go straight on

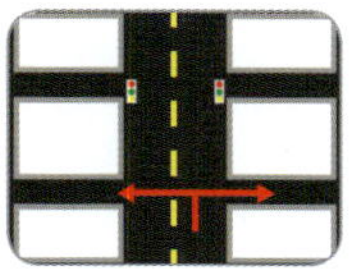

turn left/right

**6** **Write directions from your school to a place in your town. Use the words from Activity 5. Then talk to your partner.**

## GRAMMAR Have to

We can use **have to** to talk about obligation in the present, the future and the past.
We use a bare infinitive after **have to**.

*You will **have to** go to the city centre.*

*Yesterday we **had to** walk home because we missed the bus.*

**7** **Complete the sentences with the correct form of have to/don't have to.**

1 ________ he ________ get a bus now?

2 You ________ be very careful when you cross the road.

3 My library book was late and I ________ pay for it!

4 ________ you ________ buy tickets yesterday?

5 I ________ go into town, so I stayed at home.

## GRAMMAR Must

We use **must** to talk about obligation in the present and the future. We use a bare infinitive after **must**.

*You **must** buy a ticket for the bus.*

*We **mustn't** be late tomorrow.*

***Must** you make so much noise? Yes, I **must**.*

**Note:** We use **don't have to** to show that something isn't necessary but we can choose to do it if we want.

*You **don't have to** buy books – there's a library in town.*

We use **mustn't** when we want to say we are not allowed to do something.

*You **mustn't** throw rubbish in the street.*

**8** **Circle the correct words.**

1 You **have** / **must** to go round the corner.

2 When do we **have to** / **must** be at the café?

3 Did he **have to** / **must** cross the road?

4 You **mustn't** / **don't have to** go there. It's too dangerous.

5 You **mustn't** / **don't have to** work today. It's a holiday.

**9** **Listen. Write the place names.** TR: 9.4

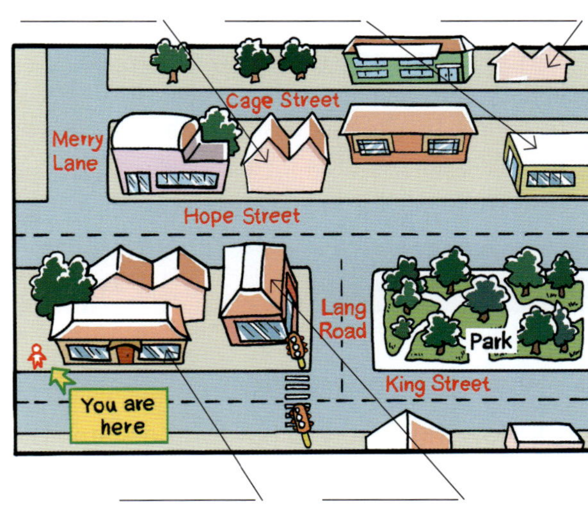


**10** **Choose two places from Activity 9. Tell your partner how to get from the first to the second place.**

**11** **Write down the directions you gave in Activity 10.**

# Lesson 2

**1** **Listen. Listen and repeat.** TR: 9.5

collection

fish

spend

ticket

try

cheap
expensive

**2** **Listen and read.** TR: 9.6

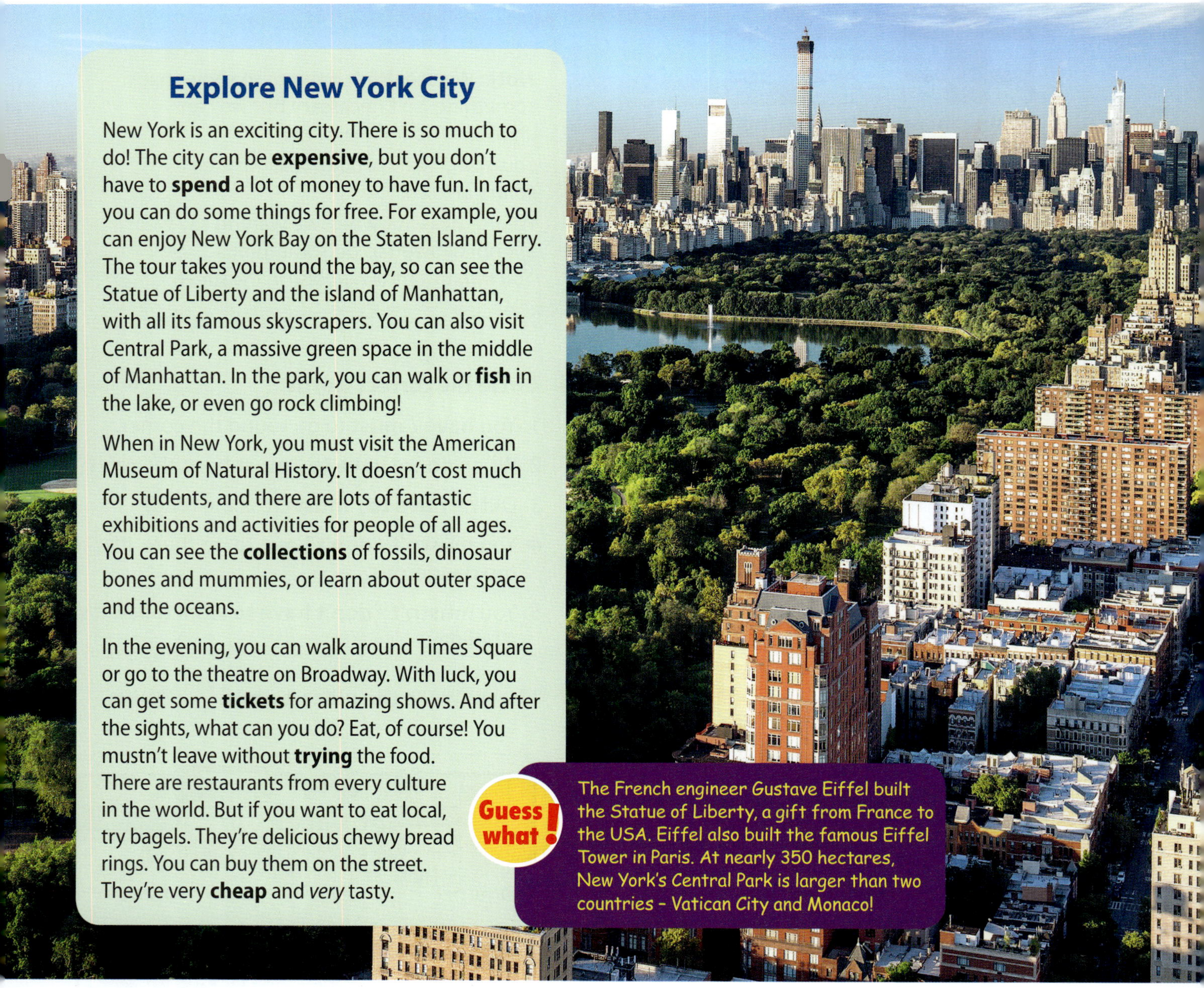

## Explore New York City

New York is an exciting city. There is so much to do! The city can be **expensive**, but you don't have to **spend** a lot of money to have fun. In fact, you can do some things for free. For example, you can enjoy New York Bay on the Staten Island Ferry. The tour takes you round the bay, so can see the Statue of Liberty and the island of Manhattan, with all its famous skyscrapers. You can also visit Central Park, a massive green space in the middle of Manhattan. In the park, you can walk or **fish** in the lake, or even go rock climbing!

When in New York, you must visit the American Museum of Natural History. It doesn't cost much for students, and there are lots of fantastic exhibitions and activities for people of all ages. You can see the **collections** of fossils, dinosaur bones and mummies, or learn about outer space and the oceans.

In the evening, you can walk around Times Square or go to the theatre on Broadway. With luck, you can get some **tickets** for amazing shows. And after the sights, what can you do? Eat, of course! You mustn't leave without **trying** the food. There are restaurants from every culture in the world. But if you want to eat local, try bagels. They're delicious chewy bread rings. You can buy them on the street. They're very **cheap** and *very* tasty.

**Guess what!**

The French engineer Gustave Eiffel built the Statue of Liberty, a gift from France to the USA. Eiffel also built the famous Eiffel Tower in Paris. At nearly 350 hectares, New York's Central Park is larger than two countries – Vatican City and Monaco!

**3** **Answer the questions.**

1. How much do you pay for the Staten Island Ferry?
2. What can you do in Central Park?
3. What types of things are in the museum's collection?
4. Where can you go to the theatre in the evening?
5. What is a bagel?

**4** **Circle the correct answers.**

1. I haven't got much money, so let's eat somewhere **cheap** / **expensive**.
2. How much money have you got to **spend** / **try**?
3. You can **fish** / **try** in the river.
4. Let's buy **tickets** / **collections** to see a concert.
5. I've got **an expensive** / **a collection** of coins.

## 5 Listen. Listen and repeat. TR: 9.7

bank

ferry

shopping centre

skyscraper

square

steps

## 6 Match.

1 bank
2 ferry
3 shopping centre
4 skyscraper
5 square
6 steps

a You sometimes go up these to enter a building.
b You go here to buy things like clothes and shoes.
c You see lots of people in this part of town.
d This is a very tall building.
e You ride on this on the water.
f You go here when you need money.

### GRAMMAR Can and could

We use **can** for the present and the future to:

**a** talk about ability.
*We **can** climb walls.*

**b** ask for and give permission.
***Can** I touch the statue, please?*
*You **can't** eat or drink in the museum.*

**c** talk about what is possible.
*You **can** walk around the park all day.*

We use **could** to talk about ability and possibility in the past.
*He **could** walk when he was one year old.*
*We **couldn't** see the theatre from the park.*
We use a bare infinitive after **can** and **could**.

## 7 Circle the correct words.

1 You **can** / **can't** visit the museum on Mondays. It's closed.
2 We **can't** / **couldn't** go to the theatre this evening.
3 I **couldn't** / **can't** go to the library yesterday because I was sick.
4 A baby **can** / **can't** go rock climbing.
5 **Could** / **Can** you walk to school last year?
6 **Can** / **Couldn't** I go out tonight, Mum?

## 8 Complete the sentences with can, can't, could or couldn't.

1 Excuse me. ____________ we ride bikes in this park?
2 We ____________ see the exhibition because the tickets were too expensive.
3 We ____________ fish with Dad when we were children.
4 Before last year Mum ____________ drive. She always used to take the bus.
5 John ____________ ride a bike. He always falls off.

## 9 Listen. Circle the correct words. TR: 9.8

1 Aunt Helen a went to Athens in **2004** / **2006**.
2 The **Parthenon** / **hotel** is on a hill in the city centre.
3 Aunt Helen a didn't visit the **Parthenon** / **museum**.
4 Dmitri is **having lunch** / **going shopping** in Plaka.
5 Dmitri isn't going to the **cinema** / **theatre**.

### SOUNDS OF ENGLISH TR: 9.9

**A** Circle the odd one out and then listen and check your answers.

| | | | |
|---|---|---|---|
| 1 | sight | right | eight |
| 2 | give | five | dive |
| 3 | wind | mind | find |
| 4 | some | come | home |

**B** Practise saying the words in A. What other words that you know rhyme with them?

# Lesson 3

**1** **Listen and read these messages to a magazine about the cities where the children live. Which of the cities would you most like to visit?** TR: 9.10

## CITY GUIDE

**Dear City Guide,**
There are two things I really like about living in Barcelona. The first is that the city is by the sea. Visitors should bring swimming costumes so that they can swim. The second is that the city is really beautiful and there are some really amazing buildings. You might spend all day walking around, so make sure you bring comfortable shoes and a camera. **Maria Cortez**

**Dear City Guide,**
I love living in Melbourne because you can meet so many people. There are people here from all over the world. Some days you might hear ten different languages! I also like the fact that you can get lots of different kinds of food. I always like to try new things to eat. **Paul Bell**

**Dear City Guide,**
One reason that I like Buenos Aires is because it's so green. There are a lot of parks and everyone goes to them often. You can go for a walk, have a picnic or go jogging. I especially love the Botanical Garden. It's got so many beautiful flowers! There are also fantastic museums, and many of them are free. The shops are brilliant, too! **Sandra Fernandez**

**2** **Write M for Maria, P for Paul or S for Sandra. Who …**

1 talks about going to the beach? ☐
2 mentions places you can visit without paying? ☐
3 talks about meeting people from different countries? ☐
4 mentions walking all day? ☐
5 mentions eating many different things? ☐
6 talks about shopping? ☐

### SAY IT LIKE THIS!

**Asking for and giving directions**

How can I get to … ?
*How can I get to the bank?*

How far is it to … ?
*How far is it to the library?*

Turn … and then …
*Turn left and then go straight ahead.*

on the right-/left-hand side
*The café is on the right-hand side of the street.*

the first/second street on the right/left
*Park Lane is the second street on the left.*

**Work with a partner. Take it in turns to ask for and give directions from your school to your house. Practise the language above.**

## GRAMMAR Might

We use **might** to talk about possibility.
*It **might** rain tomorrow.*
We use a bare infinitive after **might**.
*If you don't like noise, you **might not** have fun in the city.*

## GRAMMAR Should

We use **should** to ask for and give advice.
*You **should** be careful in the city at night.*
***Should** I turn right at Bank Street?*
We use a bare infinitive after **should**.
*They **shouldn't** talk so much during the film.*

**3 Complete the sentences with might, might not, should or shouldn't.**

1 You ______ bring an umbrella. It's cloudy.

2 We ______ arrive on time. The roads are busy.

3 ______ I bring a coat?

4 Sit down. The bus ______ be late.

5 You ______ be scared. The city is very safe.

**4 What are the people saying? Complete the sentences with the correct form of might or should.**

1

2

3

4

## WRITING Order of adjectives

**A Read about the order of adjectives.**

When we have two or more adjectives in a sentence, we put them in a certain order. We use this order:

1 **opinion** (great)
2 **size** (big)
3 **age** (old)
4 **shape** (square)
5 **colour** (red)
6 **origin** (English)
7 **material** (metal)

**B Look at these sentences. Put the adjectives in brackets in the correct order.**

1 I come from a(n) ______ (old, Spanish) town.

2 This is a ______ (green, metal, small) bookcase.

3 This is a ______ (great, Japanese, new) film.

**C Read this description of a town and put the adjectives in the correct order.**

### Scarborough

Scarborough is an (1) ______ (English, old) town by the sea. In summer, lots of people go there because it's got a (2) ______ (big, fantastic) beach. When it's sunny, you can sit on the beach or swim, but when it's cold you can watch a play in the (3) ______ (large, round) theatre or visit the (4) ______ (beautiful, stone) castle. You can buy nice sweets there, too. You can also buy (5) ______ (delicious, local) fish.

**D Write a description of a town. Use two adjectives to describe each thing. Use this plan to help you.**

**Answer these questions:**
Where is the town?
What can you do when the weather is good?
What can you do when the weather isn't good?
What can you buy/eat there?

**E Read your description and check that the adjectives are in the correct order.**

# 10 Share and Enjoy

A girl at the Olympic Rugby 7s match in Rio de Janeiro, Brazil

**1 What is the girl doing?**

1 taking a photo

2 making a film

3 watching TV

# Lesson 1

**1** **Listen. Listen and repeat.** TR: 10.1

album

print

show

comment
post
share
social media

**2** **Listen and read.** TR: 10.2

## Sharing Photos: Then and Now

**1980** I love taking photos with my new camera and **sharing** them with my friends. It's quite easy. First, I buy a roll of film and put it into the camera. I usually buy a film that takes 24 photos. When it's full, I carefully take the film out of the camera and take it to the photo shop. There, the photos are **printed**. A few days later, I go and pick them up. Some of the photos aren't great, so I throw these away. I put the good ones in an album. How do I share my photos? I take the **album** to my friend's house, and I **show** it to her. We sit down and look at the photos together.

**Today** Sharing photos? I do it all the time. Whenever I see something beautiful or something really cool happens, I take a photo. I might even just take a selfie when I haven't got anything else to take photos of. After I take a photo, I might change it in some way – put a sticker on it or change the colours. When I'm happy with the photo, I'm ready to share it. I **post** the photo on **social media** for my friends and family to see. It's fun to read everybody's **comments** on my photos. If I'm having a busy day, I might post three or four times – maybe more. Sharing photos is my favourite pastime!

**3** **Circle the correct words.**

1 It's easy to **post** / **comment** a photo on social media. Just use your smartphone.
2 People used to put photos into **an album** / **social media**. Then, they **showed** / **commented** it to their friends and family.
3 What a great photo! Can you **share** / **show** it with me, please?
4 Look at the school's **social media** / **album** page. There's lots of cool information there.
5 My mum writes **comments** / **shows** every time I post a photo to my social media page.

**4** **Read. Write T for *Then* or N for *Now*.**

1 It takes a few days to get photos from the shop. ☐
2 Photos are posted to social media. ☐
3 You can only see photos when you print them. ☐
4 Sharing photos happens straight away. ☐
5 Sharing photos only happens in person. ☐
6 People write comments on photos. ☐

## 5 Listen. Listen and repeat. TR: 10.3

| | |
|---|---|
| **app** | I've got an app on my phone that tells me how far I've walked. |
| **digital** | These digital photos look real! |
| **download** | Have you downloaded any good music lately? |
| **Internet** | When we want to know something, we can look it up on the Internet. |
| **upload** | Let's upload this photo to share on social media. |

## 6 Complete the sentences with words from Activity 5.

1 I've sent these ________ photos to you in an email.

2 First, you ________ photos to the computer. Then, you share them.

3 Mum's ________ an interesting video. Let's watch it.

4 It's too dark. Is there an ________ for a torch on this phone?

5 Kevin never reads books. He just looks everything up on the ________ .

### GRAMMAR Present simple passive

We use the passive voice:

**a** when we are more interested in the action than the person doing it.
*A lot of televisions **are made** in China.*

**b** when we don't know who does the action.
*The news **is shown** every hour.*

**c** when it is obvious who does the action.
*Television **is watched** in a lot of countries.*

If we want to talk about the person doing the action, we use **by**:
*The news **isn't read by** a local reporter.*

We make the present simple passive with **am**, **are** or **is** and the past participle of the main verb.

## 7 Complete the sentences with the present simple passive of the verbs in brackets.

1 This is an old film but it ________ (watch) by lots of young people.

2 ________ all the apps on your phone ________ (choose) by your parents?

3 This door ________ (lock) at 9 o'clock every night.

4 These comments ________ (not write) by anyone I know.

5 ________ books ________ (give) to people for free?

## 8 Complete the sentences with the present simple passive of these verbs.

not pay    not play    post    show    visit

1 A lot of adverts ________ on this app.

2 That song ________ on the radio, only on the Internet.

3 That musician ________ a lot of money.

4 ________ lots of comments ________ for this photo?

5 This social media site ________ by a lot of people.

## 9 Listen and number the pictures in the correct order. TR: 10.4

## 10 Look at the pictures in Activity 9 and tell the story in your own words, using the present simple passive.

## 11 Write a short paragraph about the story in Activity 9.

# Lesson 2

entertain
imagine
invent
programme
quality
record
technology

**1** Listen. Listen and repeat. TR: 10.5

**2** Listen and read. TR: 10.6

## Watch it!

### How showing video programmes has changed over time

What **programmes** do you watch? How do you watch them? TV has always **entertained** us and given us information, but how we watch has changed a lot.

The first electronic black and white television was **invented** in the 1920s. Back then, TV sets were very expensive. As the price came down, more people bought one. In the 1950s, colour television was shown for the first time. By the late 1960s, many people had colour TV sets.

In those days, programmes were shown only at certain times. You had to be sure you turned on the TV set, or you missed your programme. The VCR (videocassette recorder) was invented in the 1950s, and became popular in the 1970s and 1980s. VCRs allowed people to **record** a programme or film and watch it later. In the 1990s, people began watching digital films on DVDs. They were better **quality** than VCR tapes. By 1997, you could order a DVD from the Internet and it was sent to your house by post.

Now we can download TV shows and films directly to our TV sets. We even watch on our computers, tablets and phones. This **technology** continues to improve. Just **imagine** how we'll be watching in 100 years. People say that 3D TV and virtual reality – which makes you feel like you're actually there – are the future. Whatever it is, we'll be watching!

**Guess what!** The first TV advert was shown in 1941. It was for a watch. The advert cost the watch company $9 to make.

**3** Read and tick T for *True* or F for *False*.

1 Colour TV sets were invented in the 1920s. T F

2 Most people had a VCR by the 1950s. T F

3 Digital films on DVD are better quality than films on VCR tapes. T F

4 In 100 years, we'll probably still watch programmes and films in the same way as we do today. T F

**4** Match the words to their meanings.

1 quality
2 record
3 entertain
4 technology
5 imagine
6 invent
7 programme

a Something on TV
b An exciting new development
c What you do if you want to watch something later
d Make for the first time
e Help people have fun
f How good or bad something is
g Have an idea about something

## 5 Listen. Listen and repeat. TR: 10.7

| | |
|---|---|
| **cartoon** | Many children like watching cartoons on TV. |
| **documentary** | This is an interesting documentary about giraffes. |
| **news** | My parents always watch the evening news. |
| **reality show** | We're going to be on a reality show. It will be filmed at our house. |
| **series** | This is the first programme of the series. |
| **sitcom** | My favourite sitcom is shown every Thursday at eight o'clock. |

## 6 Circle the odd one out.

| | | | |
|---|---|---|---|
| 1 | news | documentary | album |
| 2 | app | programme | cartoon |
| 3 | technology | invent | reality show |
| 4 | comment | film | documentary |
| 5 | sitcom | information | entertain |

### GRAMMAR Past simple passive

We make the past simple passive with **was** or **were** and the past participle of the main verb.

## 7 Complete the sentences with the past simple passive of the verbs in brackets.

1 That series __________ (show) for ten years.

2 My cousin __________ (choose) for a reality show last year.

3 A lot of actors __________ (interview) for the job.

4 This documentary __________ (not make) in London.

5 Why __________ a reporter __________ (not send) to the scene?

## 8 Listen. Tick the correct pictures. TR: 10.8

1 What happened in Carneiros Beach yesterday afternoon?

2 How did the boy help the family?

3 What's the weather going to be like this afternoon?

4 Who will read the news tomorrow morning?

### SOUNDS OF ENGLISH TR: 10.9

**A** Read these pairs of words. Write **S** if they sound the same and **D** if they sound different.

| | | | |
|---|---|---|---|
| 1 | see | she | ☐ |
| 2 | there | their | ☐ |
| 3 | knows | nose | ☐ |
| 4 | Phil | feel | ☐ |
| 5 | wear | where | ☐ |

**B** Listen and check your answers.

# Lesson 3

**1** **Listen and read about an Internet star. Who's your favourite Internet star?** TR: 10.10

Do you watch many videos that people post online? People post different types of videos, showing their pets or a special talent, for example. If the video is interesting or funny, others share it. That might happen over and over. Before long, the videos can get a lot of followers. Suddenly, even if they don't want to be, the people in them become Internet stars!

This happened to Evan. With his father's help, Evan began making videos in 2011, when he was just six years old. Now, his online channel has got over 1.3 million followers. People – mostly children – have watched his videos more than 1.2 billion times!

Why do so many children like Evan's videos? His father says it's because children feel like Evan is their friend. The videos are funny and interesting. Some show Evan's adventures with his younger sister, Jillian. But it's Evan's toy reviews that made him famous. He plays with the toys and says what he likes about them. Many toy companies have come to Evan with new toys for him to review. Evan has been in TV adverts for toys. And Evan and Jillian have even been voices on a cartoon.

Companies pay the family for adverts on Evan's channel. But to them, it's not about the money. Evan saves everything he earns for college, and he gives away most of the toys he reviews. Smart, generous and funny – it's no wonder Evan is so popular!

**2** **Circle the letter for the correct answer.**

1 Evan began making videos when he was ____ .
   a six   b eleven
2 Evan's channel has got over ____ followers.
   a 1.2 billion   b 1.3 million
3 Toy companies ask Evan to ____ their toys.
   a review   b record
4 Evan and Jillian have been ____ .
   a toy makers   b voices in a cartoon
5 Evan ____ most of the toys from his videos.
   a keeps   b gives away

**SAY IT LIKE THIS!**

**Expressing preferences**

My favourite … is …
*__My favourite__ Internet star __is__ Evan.*
Do you prefer … to … ?
*__Do you prefer__ Internet videos __to__ television?*
I prefer … to …
*I __prefer__ films __to__ television.*
I can't stand …
*I __can't stand__ adverts.*

**Talk about your preferences in videos with a partner.**

## 3 Listen. Tick the sentences that are true. TR: 10.11

1 Raj plays the guitar. ☐
2 Alisa follows Raj on the Internet. ☐
3 Raj posts a hundred videos a week. ☐
4 Raj posts only his songs. ☐
5 Raj's followers prefer music. ☐
6 Raj can't stand reading bad comments. ☐

## 4 Discuss these questions with a partner.

1 How often do you watch TV programmes?
2 What types of programmes do you prefer?
3 What other things do you use to watch videos?
4 How many hours a week do you watch videos/TV?
5 Do your parents use social media? If so, do they post photos or videos of you?
6 Do you know someone with an Internet video channel? What's it like?
7 How do you usually watch films – in the cinema, on TV, on a tablet or on a phone? What do you prefer?

## WRITING Spelling mistakes

### A There's one spelling mistake in each sentence. Find it and correct it.

1 This Internet radio station is awfull.
2 I thing reality shows are interesting.
3 Those tablits in the adverts are expensive.
4 We watch sitcomms after dinner.
5 He prefers watching realy funny shows.
6 They always watch cartons on Saturday mornings.
7 My friends and I lisen to Internet radio.
8 My sister was on the new TV programe.

### B Look at the review of a television programme below. Find eight spelling mistakes and correct them.

My favourite TV programme is a reality show called *Danger Island*. It isn't on TV at the moment, but it starts again in autum.

In the show, people are sent to an island. They have to sleep outside, without any tents. They can only take one thing with them. People usualy choose something necessary, like a toothbrush. The people also have to find food. They spend a lot of time fishing and collecting frut from the trees. After every show, one person has to leeve. At the end, there are only two peple on the island and one of them is chozen as the winner.

I really like *Danger Island* because it's very exciting. Sometimes people have to do really dangerous things, like get around snakes or climb high rocks. I thing it really entertans you when you watch it. I don't want to be on the show, however. I like living in a house!

### C Write a review of your favourite television programme or Internet channel. Use this plan to help you.

**Paragraph 1**
Say what your favourite programme or Internet channel is. If you choose the TV programme, say what day/time it's shown.

**Paragraph 2**
Say what happens on the show/channel.

**Paragraph 3**
Say why you like the show/channel.

### D Read your review and check that you have spelt everything correctly.

# Review

## 1 Label the photos.

______

______

______

______

______

______

## 2 Circle the odd one out.

| | | | |
|---|---|---|---|
| 1 | shopping centre | channel | bank |
| 2 | reality show | ferry | news |
| 3 | directions | collection | information |
| 4 | go straight on | turn left | upload |
| 5 | entertain | inform | invent |
| 6 | expensive | cheap | follow |

## 3 Circle the correct words.

1 Sarita took lots of photos. She's **uploading** / **inventing** them now. Then, she'll **post** / **spend** them on her social media page.

2 Years ago, people used to share photos by sitting together and looking at **comments** / **an album**.

3 I can't **imagine** / **entertain** how difficult it was to build that tall skyscraper!

4 To get to the library entrance, you have to climb **the steps** / **around the corner**.

## 4 Give directions from your classroom to the school's front door. Use the words in the box.

go past   go straight on   steps   turn right/left

## 5 Choose the correct answers.

1 You ____ to leave your car here and walk to the shopping centre.
  a have   b must   c can

2 We ____ watch the news. Let's watch a sitcom instead.
  a can't   b mustn't   c don't have to

3 ____ I turn left at the library?
  a Might   b Should   c Have

4 You ____ go to the theatre early or you won't find any cheap tickets.
  a have   b can   c must

5 You ____ miss this TV programme. It's great!
  a might   b shouldn't   c don't have to

6 We ____ go on the ferry tomorrow, but we haven't decided yet.
  a must   b might   c have to

## 6 Complete Farah's conversation with her grandma. Use these words.

can   can't   couldn't   have to
might   might not   should   shouldn't

**G:** You (1) ______________ watch so many videos. I didn't watch a lot of videos when I was young.

**F:** You (2) ______________ watch TV because you didn't have a TV set or a computer!

**G:** That's true, but you (3) ______________ be outside in the fresh air. It's good for you.

**F:** I (4) ______________ go outside. It's cold.

**G:** It isn't cold! You (5) ______________ be very warm, but you'll be OK with a coat on. You can go to the cinema. There (6) ______________ be a good film on.

**F:** But I (7) ______________ watch a film here for free. The cinema is expensive.

**G:** Oh, dear. Yes, it is.

**F:** OK, I'm sorry but I (8) ______________ stay at home today. I wanted to watch a short film, and then I'll do my homework.

**7 Change the verbs in bold into the passive voice to complete the second sentences in each pair.**

1 Dean **gave** me some new music
I ________ some new music by Dean.

2 They **make** a lot of funny adverts for TV.
A lot of funny adverts ________ for TV.

3 John Logie Baird **invented** the TV, didn't he?
The TV ________ by John Logie Baird, wasn't it?

4 The studio **doesn't pay** its actors much.
The actors ________ much by the studio.

5 In the film, the man **follows** the police officer.
In the film, the police officer ________ by the man.

6 They **showed** us round the museum.
We ________ round the museum.

**8 Think of a new technology. Write three sentences about it. Use the passive voice.**

________

________

________

________

________

## Song TR: 10.12

We're flying today far across the sea
To amazing New York, New York.
There's so much to do,
there's so much to see
In amazing New York, New York.

We must see the Statue of Liberty
In amazing New York, New York.
If the tickets are cheap,
we'll see a comedy
In amazing New York, New York.

Before it gets dark we'll go to Central Park.
We can picnic or climb up a rock
You don't have to pay
to sail round New York Bay
We'll see the sights or we'll go for a walk.
In amazing New York, New York.

# Video

## 1 BEFORE YOU WATCH

**You're going to spend the day in town with your friends. Where can you go? Circle.**

the town square
the museum
the park
a shopping centre
a skyscraper

My friends and I ______________________.

**Now describe what you and your friends are going to do in town.**

We're going to the museum to look at art.

We're going to go cycling in the park.

## 2 WORDS TO KNOW

**Match the words to the pictures.**

painting    painter    neighbourhood    writer

______________

______________

______________

______________

## 3 WHILE YOU WATCH

**There are so many places to see in Paris! How many museums are there in the video?**

## 4 AFTER YOU WATCH

**Tick T for *True* or F for *False*.**

1 You can see paintings at the Musee D'Orsay. T F

2 You can walk from the Tuileries Gardens to the Louvre. T F

3 You can't go to the top of the Eiffel Tower. T F

4 You can only see statues at the Louvre. T F

5 The Palais Garnier is a theatre where you can see opera. T F

## 5 WATCH AGAIN

**Talk about what you must do in Paris when you visit.**

You must visit the Eiffel Tower!

Cool! I love art.

Then you must go to the Louvre, too.

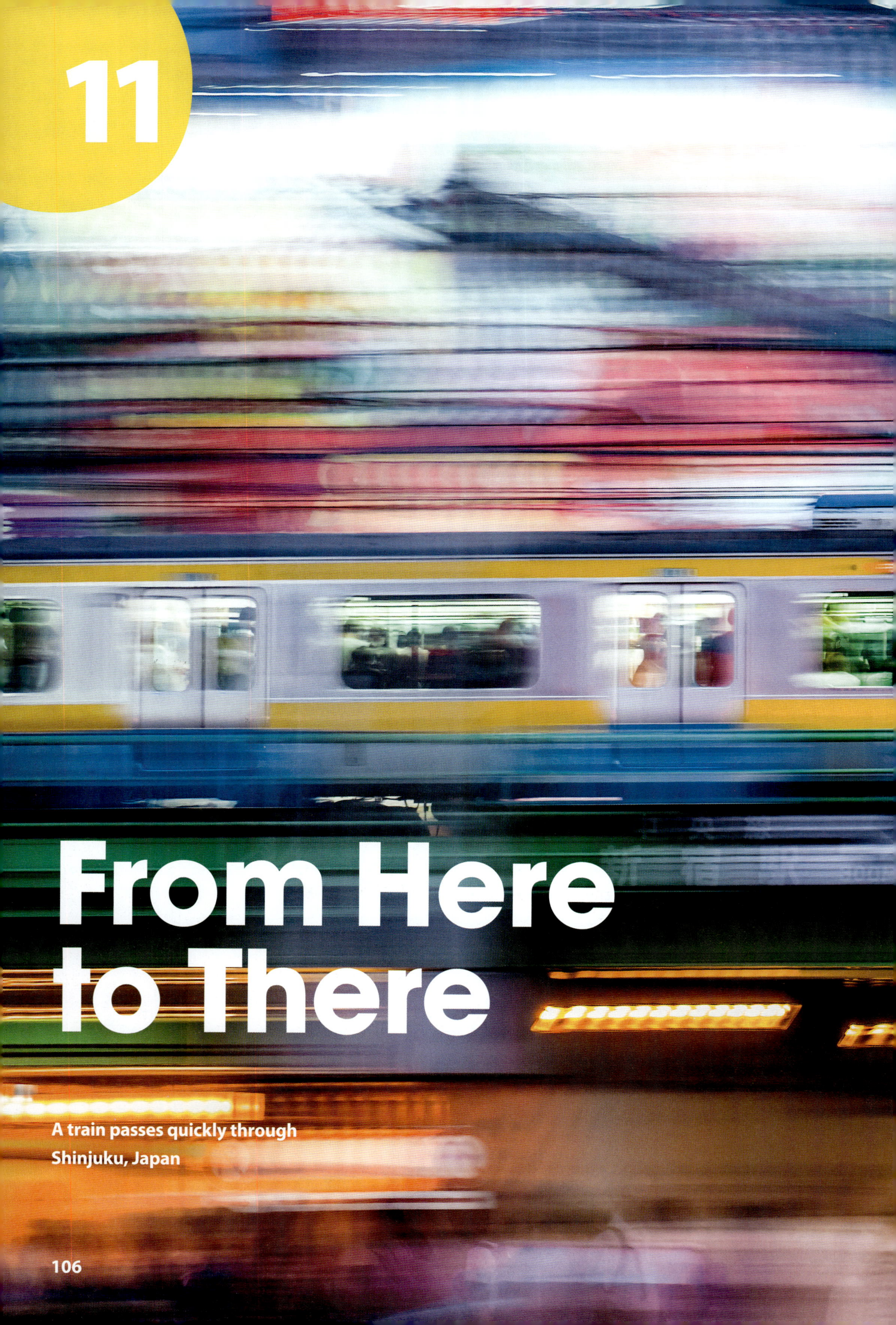

11

# From Here to There

A train passes quickly through Shinjuku, Japan

**1 Look at the photo. Answer the questions.**

1 Is this train going fast or slow?

2 What types of transport do you take?

# Lesson 1

**1** **Listen. Listen and repeat.** TR: 11.1

destination

get on

get off

parking

pedestrian

traffic

**2** **Listen and read.** TR: 11.2

## Car-free Cities?

**Traffic** is a big problem around the world. In Los Angeles, USA, people spend 90 hours a year in traffic. It's worse in Rio de Janeiro, Brazil, at 100 hours per year. The worst is Mexico City. Residents there lose over 200 hours each year. And drivers in the UK spend more than 100 days of their lives looking for **parking**!

Many cities want to improve transport. Planners in Helsinki, Finland, want to make cars unnecessary by 2025. They're creating an app to let users find the best transport for their trip, including buses, trains, shared bikes, ferries and taxis. The user enters a location and **destination**, and the app plans the trip using the best types of transport. This will be faster and cheaper.

Helsinki has also got more than 1,200 km (745 mi.) of bike lanes. There's a huge bus system with over 1,000 bus stops. There are trams and underground trains. There's even a new minibus service. People **get on** wherever they are, and **get off** right at their destination, instead of at a bus stop. Many of the roads in the town centre are for **pedestrians** only, so no traffic is allowed.

Will this work? Possibly. Younger people want simple, cheap transport that's green – not cars. By 2025, Helsinki will surely have fewer cars, and it may just be car-free!

**3** **Complete the sentences with words from Activity 1.**

1 Dad's going to be late because he can't find a ____________ space.

2 This is a ____________ street. No cars are allowed.

3 It's been a long journey. I can't wait to get to my ____________ .

4 We're here. It's time to ____________ the train.

5 There's lots of ____________ on the roads at six o'clock.

**4** **Read. Tick T for *True* or F for *False*.**

1 The worst traffic in the world is in Los Angeles, USA. T F

2 Planners in Helsinki are making it easier to get around the city. T F

3 The app they're planning will only find buses or taxis. T F

4 Helsinki has got lots of bike lanes and pedestrian streets. T F

5 At the moment, people need a car to get around Helsinki. T F

6 Young people are looking for cheaper cars because they think they need them. T F

## 5 Listen. Listen and repeat. TR: 11.3

bus stop

driver

bike lane

tram

motorbike

scooter

## 6 Write the word from Activity 5 that matches each description.

1 This has two wheels and is often big and loud ______

2 You can ride your bike here ______

3 The person controlling the car ______

4 You wait here for the bus ______

5 This is a type of train ______

6 This has two small wheels ______

### GRAMMAR Comparatives and superlatives

We use the comparative form to compare two or more people, animals or things. We often use the word **than** after the comparative form.

We add **-er** to short adjectives.
*A bus is **faster than** a bicycle.*

We don't add **-er** to long adjectives, but we use the word **more** before the adjective.
*Travelling by train is **more interesting than** travelling by boat.*

We can use (**not**) **as** + adjective + **as** to compare two things.
*The bus is **as cheap as** the tram.*
*This seat **isn't as comfortable as** that one.*

We use the superlative form to compare a person, an animal or thing with many other people, animals or things. We add **-est** to short adjectives and use the word **the** before the adjective.
*These tickets are **the cheapest**.*

We don't add **-est** to long adjectives, but we use the word **most** before the adjective.
*These tickets are **the most expensive**.*

Look at these irregular forms:

| Adjective | Comparative | Superlative |
| --- | --- | --- |
| good | **better** | **the best** |
| bad | **worse** | **the worst** |

## 7 Complete the sentences with the correct comparative or superlative form.

1 A ferry is ______ (fast) than a bus.

2 I never walk anywhere. I'm ______ (lazy) person in our family.

3 Planes are ______ (exciting) than trains.

4 This bike is ______ (not nice) as that one.

5 Is the tram ______ (popular) means of transport in Helsinki?

## 8 Complete the sentences with the correct comparative or superlative structure.

big good frightening slow

1 

This is ______ journey I've ever had!

2 

Why is his seat ______ mine?

3 

The weather isn't ______ it was yesterday.

4 

This is ______ car in the world.

## 9 Listen. Circle the correct words. TR: 11.4

1 Fausto is going to Lisbon with his **parents** / **grandparents**.

2 Fausto thinks the **train** / **coach** is more exciting.

3 The coach isn't as **fast** / **long** as the train.

4 Train tickets are **15 €** / **30 €** each.

5 In the end, Fausto thinks they should go by **train** / **coach**.

## 10 Work with a partner. Compare the means of transport using the words in brackets.

a plane and ferry (expensive)

b bicycle and motorbike (fast)

c train and coach (comfortable)

## 11 Write three sentences comparing the items in Activity 10.

# Lesson 2

**1** Listen. Listen and repeat. TR: 11.5

display

escalator

gallery

passenger

track

billion

**2** Listen and read. TR: 11.6

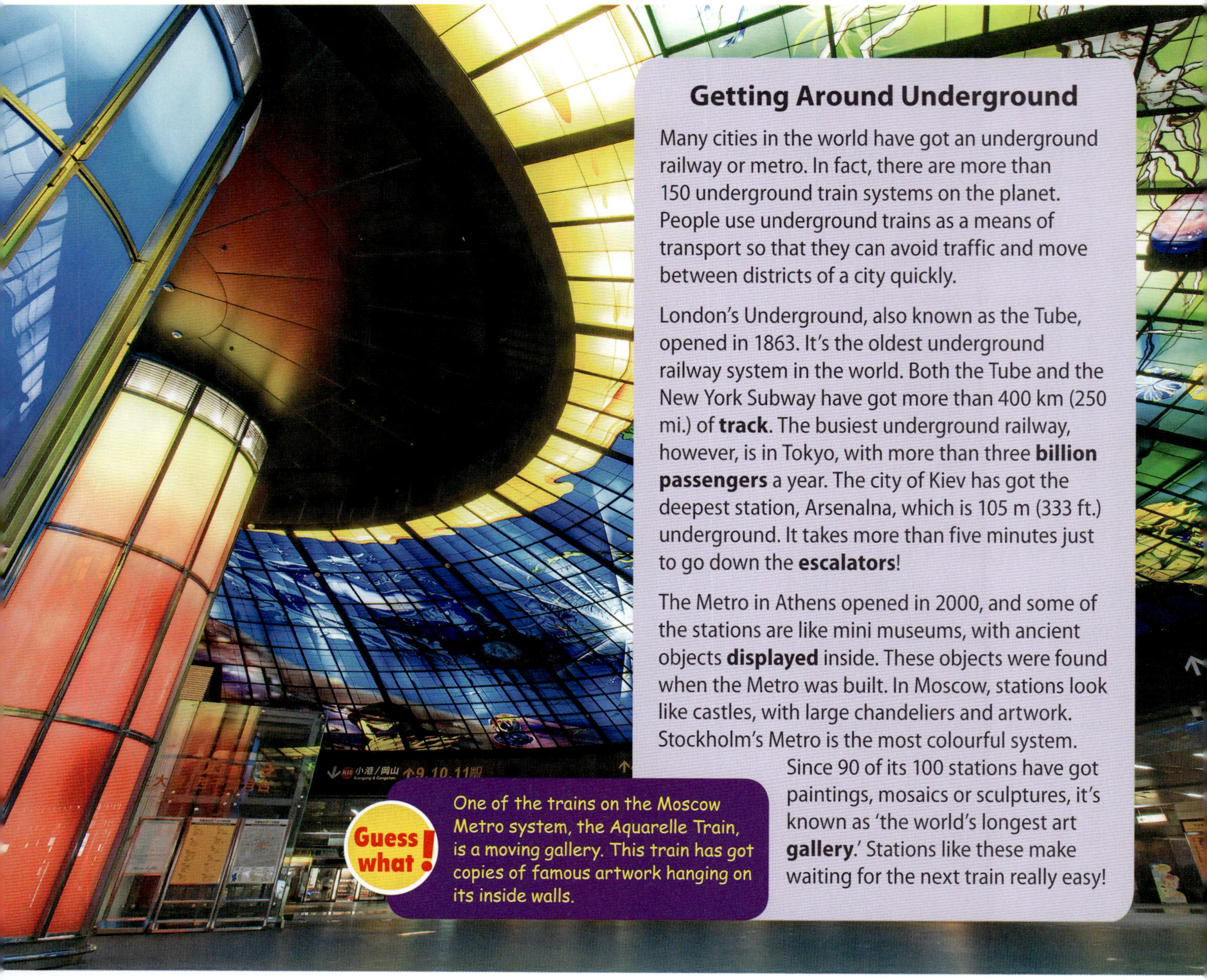

## Getting Around Underground

Many cities in the world have got an underground railway or metro. In fact, there are more than 150 underground train systems on the planet. People use underground trains as a means of transport so that they can avoid traffic and move between districts of a city quickly.

London's Underground, also known as the Tube, opened in 1863. It's the oldest underground railway system in the world. Both the Tube and the New York Subway have got more than 400 km (250 mi.) of **track**. The busiest underground railway, however, is in Tokyo, with more than three **billion passengers** a year. The city of Kiev has got the deepest station, Arsenalna, which is 105 m (333 ft.) underground. It takes more than five minutes just to go down the **escalators**!

The Metro in Athens opened in 2000, and some of the stations are like mini museums, with ancient objects **displayed** inside. These objects were found when the Metro was built. In Moscow, stations look like castles, with large chandeliers and artwork. Stockholm's Metro is the most colourful system. Since 90 of its 100 stations have got paintings, mosaics or sculptures, it's known as 'the world's longest art **gallery**.' Stations like these make waiting for the next train really easy!

**Guess what!** One of the trains on the Moscow Metro system, the Aquarelle Train, is a moving gallery. This train has got copies of famous artwork hanging on its inside walls.

**3** Answer the questions.

1 Where is the oldest underground train system?
2 Which underground railway has got the most passengers?
3 What is the name of the deepest station in the world?
4 When did the Athens Metro open?
5 What is the Stockholm metro known as?

**4** Match the word with its meaning.

1 billion
2 display
3 track
4 escalator
5 passenger

a This is a person going somewhere on any type of transport.
b Trains run on this.
c This is a very large number.
d This is a moving staircase.
e You do this when you show things to people.

## 5 Listen. Listen and repeat. TR: 11.7

inspector

lift

loudspeaker

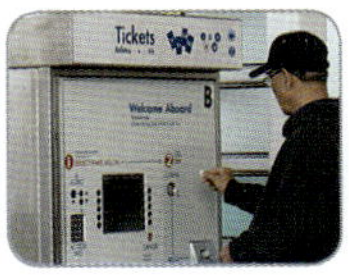
ticket machine

timetable

## 6 Complete the sentences with words from Activity 5.

1 I heard over the ______________ that the train to Kiev is late.

2 Do you want to take the ______________ or the escalator to get to the platform?

3 Does the ______________ take credit cards?

4 Please hurry. This ______________ says that the bus will arrive in three minutes!

5 Let's get our tickets out. The ______________ is coming to check them.

### GRAMMAR Both, either, neither

We use **both**, **either** and **neither** to talk about two people, animals or things.

We use **both** with affirmative verbs. It means *one and the other.*
*I have travelled by* ***both*** *train* ***and*** *bus.*
***Both*** *cities have got good railways.*

We use **either** with affirmative and negative verbs. It means *one or the other.* It is followed by **or** or **of**.
*You can use* ***either*** *a ticket* ***or*** *a travel card.*
*I can't use* ***either of*** *these means of transport.*

We use **neither** with affirmative verbs, but it has got a negative meaning. It means not one and not the other. It is followed by **nor** or **of**.
***Neither*** *a taxi* ***nor*** *a car is a good choice.*
***Neither of*** *the trams was on time.*

## 7 Circle the correct words.

1 I won't get on **either** / **neither** of these trains.

2 **Neither** / **Both** a bus nor a bike is very fast.

3 Take **both** / **either** the escalator or the lift.

4 **Both** / **Either** passengers have got a seat.

## 8 Complete the sentences with both, either or neither.

1 ______________ my car nor John's is blue.

2 I've never been on ______________ a plane or a tram.

3 We'll use the stairs because ______________ the escalator and the lift are broken.

4 ______________ of the boys like buses, but they like cars.

5 ______________ the Kiev and the Moscow Metro have deep stations.

## 9 Listen to Lena and Guy talking about a new car. Tick T for *True* and F for *False*. TR: 11.8

| | | | |
|---|---|---|---|
| 1 | Lena's mum has got a new car. | T | F |
| 2 | The car is small. | T | F |
| 3 | The car is more expensive than other cars. | T | F |
| 4 | The car is fast. | T | F |
| 5 | You can only get the car in blue, red or black. | T | F |
| 6 | Lena's dad wants a new car. | T | F |

## 10 Discuss the following in pairs.

1 Compare two types of transport that you often take.

2 Have you taken an underground train? Where?

3 Describe a train or bus station that you know about or have been to.

### SOUNDS OF ENGLISH TR: 11.9

**A** Read these pairs of words. What is the difference in the sound of **th** in each pair?

1 **th**is, **th**in

2 ei**th**er, bo**th**

3 **th**ere, **th**ing

**B** Now put these words in the correct column. Listen and check.

bath neither other thank

| bro**th**er | too**th** |
|---|---|
| ______________ | ______________ |
| ______________ | ______________ |

# Lesson 3

**1 Listen and read these entries in a travel guide. Which transport sounds most exciting to you?**
TR: 11.10

## TRAVEL GUIDE

### Venice, Italy

In Venice, there are buses and taxis just like any other city but they travel on water instead of roads! The water bus is called the Vaporetto and it works just like an ordinary bus. You can get a single ticket, a ticket to travel for 1–3 days or a weekly pass. Some visitors like riding in gondolas, but they're too expensive for others. It doesn't really matter, however. The Vaporettos and the water taxis aren't as romantic as gondolas, but they're good enough for getting around, and they run every day.

### San Francisco, USA

In San Francisco getting around is really easy – there are all kinds of transport: buses, underground trains and shared cars and bikes. The oldest and the best, however, are the cable cars. Some of them are modern but others are just like the cable cars that used to be in the city a hundred years ago. You can use special tickets for all means of transport for 90 minutes, and they're not too expensive. Some people think that walking in the city is too difficult because of the hills. Cable cars are a fun way to get up and down the city's steep hills!

### Medellin, Colombia

Medellin is becoming a popular tourist destination. People come for the museums, gardens and its huge aquarium. But the top tourist attraction in Medellin is actually a means of transport: the Medellin Metrocable. The Metrocable has more than 30,000 riders each day on its three lines, many of them tourists. It's a great way to get a beautiful view of the city from above. The Metrocable is part of the city's larger Metro system, which lets you explore the entire city underground or in the sky. The tickets are very inexpensive, too!

**2 Tick T for *True* or F for *False*.**

1 The gondolas in Venice are cheap enough for everyone. T F
2 In San Francisco, you can travel on different means of transport with one ticket. T F
3 There are lots of hills in San Francisco. T F
4 The aquarium is Medellin's most popular tourist attraction. T F
5 You can use one ticket to explore Medellin underground and in the sky. T F

### SAY IT LIKE THIS!

**Talking about transport**

How can I get to … ?
You can take the tram/bus from the stop/station.
*Excuse me, how can I get to Richmond Park?*
*You can take the tram from the stop over there.*

Can I buy a single/return ticket / buy a travel pass?
Single/Return tickets / Travel passes cost …
*Can I buy a travel pass, please?*
*Yes. Travel passes cost 8 € for one week.*

Where do I get on/off the tram/bus/metro?
*Where do I get off the bus?*
*You get off the bus at Central Square.*

**Talk to your partner about transport.**

## GRAMMAR Too and enough

We use **too** to show that there is more of something than we need and that this is a problem. It is followed by an adjective.
*The bus is **too slow**, so let's get the metro.*

We use **enough** to show that there is as much of something as we need. It comes after an adjective.
*I've washed the car.*
*Is it **clean enough** now?*

We can also use **enough** before uncountable nouns and plural countable nouns to show that there is less of something than we need and that this is a problem.
*I didn't have **enough money** for a taxi.*
*Did we buy **enough tickets** for everyone?*

**3 Complete the sentences with too or enough.**

1 I won't buy that car. It's ______________ old.

2 The bus isn't fast ______________ . Let's walk.

3 Have we got ______________ money for the tickets?

4 You can't go alone. You're ______________ young.

5 Are there ______________ seats for all the passengers?

## WRITING Headings

**A Read about headings.**

When we write reports, we often use headings above each part. The headings tell us what each part is about so we can find the information we need easily.

**B Read the report and match these headings with each paragraph.**

a Which means of transport is the best?
b Kinds of transport
c Cost
d Problems

### Around China: Getting from Shanghai to Beijing

The distance between Shanghai to Beijing is 1,200 km (745 mi.). You can drive from one city to the other. There are also more than 50 flights between the cities each day. Or you can take a high-speed train. It takes about 5 hours.

Train tickets cost about 75€ per person for second class. First class are more expensive: about 125€. Aeroplane ticket prices are different. The airline and the dates can change the prices. They're usually more expensive than the train or driving.

Driving takes a long time – usually more than 12 hours. There are roads that cost money, and there's lots of traffic. Flying can be expensive, and flights can be late or cancelled, depending on the weather. It seems quicker, but people often spend a long time in airports, and lots of money getting to and from airports.

As it's cheaper than flying and faster than driving, I think taking the high-speed train is the best way to get from Shanghai to Beijing at the moment.

**C Write a report about transport in your area. Use this plan to help you.**

**Answer the questions.**

**Paragraph 1**
What kinds of public transport are there in your area?

**Paragraph 2**
How much do the tickets cost?

**Paragraph 3**
What problems are there?

**Paragraph 4**
Conclusion: Which is the best means of transport?

**D Check that you have used the correct headings for each part of your report.**

# 12 Jobs

The Yasur volcano, Tanna Island, Vanuatu

**1 Look at the photo. Answer the questions.**

1 What's this man doing?

2 What do you think his job is?

# Lesson 1

check
patient

customer
queue

opinion
skill

**1** **Listen. Listen and repeat.** TR: 12.1

**2** **Listen and read.** TR: 12.2

## You Do What?!

What job do you want to have when you get older? A doctor? A police officer? Or are you looking for something different? If so, you might want to think about these unusual jobs.

### Water-Slide Tester

If you like water slides, this might be the job for you. You get to travel to waterparks around the world and try out their newest slides. The job sounds like it's all fun, but testers are also **checking** for safety. So, this job can be dangerous. You also need to have social media **skills**. After each test, you must post your **opinion** about the slide on social media. To get this job, you must be fun-loving and crazy about waterparks!

### Queue-sitter

Are you a very **patient** person? Are you happy to spend an afternoon waiting at the bank or tax office? If so, you could easily be a **queue**-sitter. One queue-sitter in Italy earns 10€ an hour patiently waiting in queues for his **customers**. 'I am the person who will wait in line for those who don't have the time or desire,' he says.

### Food taster

Food companies look for people with a strong sense of smell and taste to help them create new food products. Some tasters try a lot of different types of food. Others just taste one type of food, like ice cream. One ice-cream taster says she might taste up to 250 flavours in a day. After work, she goes for walks to stay healthy!

**3** **Write the word.**

1 What you think about something

___ ___ ___ n ___ ___ ___

2 Happy to wait for something

___ ___ ___ ___ ___ ___ t

3 To look at something carefully

___ h ___ ___ ___

4 A group of people in a line, waiting

___ ___ e ___ ___

5 A special ability

___ ___ ___ l ___

**4** **Write the job being described — water-slide tester (WST), queue-sitter (QS) or food taster (FT).**

1 You must be a very patient person. ______

2 You must like travelling. ______

3 You must have a strong sense of taste. ______

4 You must be happy to get wet. ______

5 You work with scientists. ______

6 You save people time. ______

## 5 Listen. Listen and repeat. TR: 12.3

artist

chef

detective

mechanic

reporter

sailor

## 6 Write the job for which each item is needed.

1  ______________

2  ______________

3  ______________

4  ______________

5  ______________

6  ______________

### GRAMMAR Adverbs of manner

We use adverbs of manner to describe how we do something. We make most adverbs by adding **-ly** to the adjective, but if the adjective ends in **-y**, we take off the **-y** and add **-ily**:

| Adjective | Adverb |
|---|---|
| quick | quick**ly** |
| lazy | laz**ily** |

*The artist paints **beautifully**.*
*The detective caught the thief **easily**.*

Some adverbs are irregular:

| Adjective | Adverb |
|---|---|
| hard | hard |
| fast | fast |
| high | high |
| right | right |
| wrong | wrong |
| good | well |

## 7 Complete the sentences with adverbs made from the adjectives in brackets.

1 The doctor arrived ______________ (quick).
2 'Talk ______________ (slow)! I can't understand you!' said the detective.
3 That chef cooks really ______________ (good).
4 Sam is a sailor. He doesn't swim ______________ (bad).
5 Grandad worked ______________ (hard) for many years as a mechanic.
6 The taxi driver was driving ______________ (fast) and I was scared.
7 The detective smiled ______________ (happy) when he caught the man.

## 8 Listen to four people talking about their jobs. Draw lines from the speakers to the pictures. Then write the job underneath. TR: 12.4

Speaker 1

Speaker 2

Speaker 3

Speaker 4

a 
______________

b 
______________

c 
______________

d 
______________

## 9 Role-play one of the jobs from this lesson. Ask and answer these questions with your partner.

How interesting/boring/easy/difficult is the job?
When do you have to work?
What do you like/dislike about the work?

## 10 Write a short paragraph about the job you described in Activity 9.

# Lesson 2

**1** **Listen. Listen and repeat.** TR: 12.5

author

designer

day off
focus on
full-time/part-time job

**2** **Listen. Listen and read.** TR: 12.6

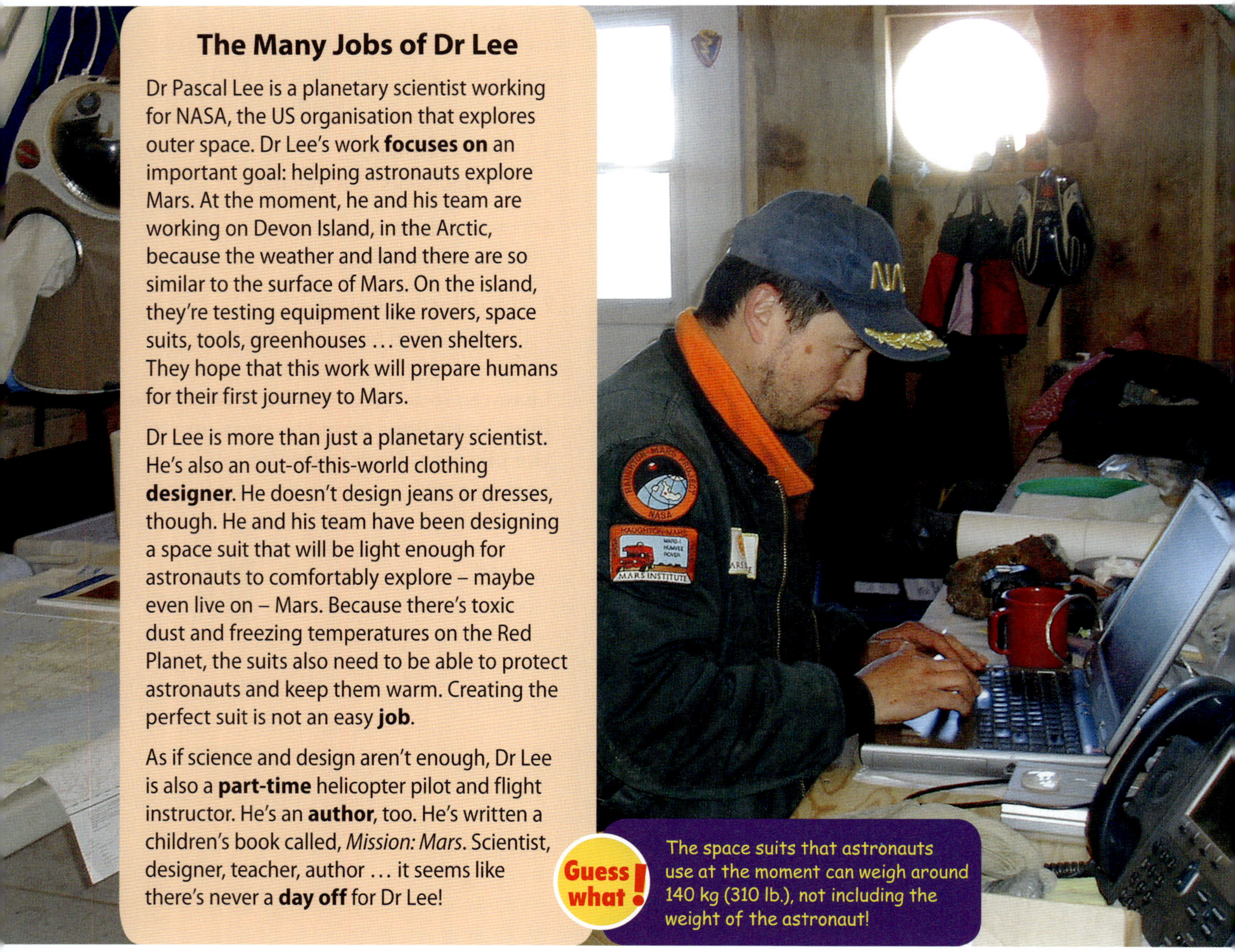

## The Many Jobs of Dr Lee

Dr Pascal Lee is a planetary scientist working for NASA, the US organisation that explores outer space. Dr Lee's work **focuses on** an important goal: helping astronauts explore Mars. At the moment, he and his team are working on Devon Island, in the Arctic, because the weather and land there are so similar to the surface of Mars. On the island, they're testing equipment like rovers, space suits, tools, greenhouses … even shelters. They hope that this work will prepare humans for their first journey to Mars.

Dr Lee is more than just a planetary scientist. He's also an out-of-this-world clothing **designer**. He doesn't design jeans or dresses, though. He and his team have been designing a space suit that will be light enough for astronauts to comfortably explore – maybe even live on – Mars. Because there's toxic dust and freezing temperatures on the Red Planet, the suits also need to be able to protect astronauts and keep them warm. Creating the perfect suit is not an easy **job**.

As if science and design aren't enough, Dr Lee is also a **part-time** helicopter pilot and flight instructor. He's an **author**, too. He's written a children's book called, *Mission: Mars*. Scientist, designer, teacher, author … it seems like there's never a **day off** for Dr Lee!

**Guess what!** The space suits that astronauts use at the moment can weigh around 140 kg (310 lb.), not including the weight of the astronaut!

**3** **Read and tick T for *True* or F for *False*.**

1 Dr Lee's work only focuses on exploring the Arctic. T F
2 Dr Lee and his team are testing equipment in the Arctic. T F
3 People have already travelled to Mars. T F
4 Dr Lee designs jeans and dresses. T F
5 Dr Lee is a part-time pilot and author. T F

**4** **Circle the correct words.**

1 I've got a **day off** / **part-time job** on Wednesday.
2 The project **designs** / **focuses on** using the new technology.
3 The **author** / **designer** of this book lives nearby.
4 My mum works ten hours a week at her **full-time job** / **part-time job**.
5 Carol is a clothing **author** / **designer**.
6 Victor is looking for a new **job** / **day off**, but he can't find one.

## 5 Listen. Listen and repeat. TR: 12.7

| | |
|---|---|
| **career** | She's got an interesting career as a costume designer. |
| **employee** | There are 300 employees working here. |
| **experience** | Have you got experience writing blogs? |
| **manager** | You must ask the manager for a day off. |
| **staff** | Everybody on the staff is helpful. |

## 6 Complete the message with words from Activity 5.

Dear Sir or Madam,

I recently saw a posting for a job as a(n) (1) ______________ . I have worked in an office for seven years, so I've got a lot of (2) ______________ . At the moment I manage 14 members of (3) ______________ in a car company. I've been a(n) (4) ______________ here since 2017, but I'm now interested in a new (5) ______________ with your company.

### GRAMMAR Relative clauses

We use relative clauses to give more information about people, animals and things. A relative clause begins with a relative pronoun or adverb. We use **who** for people, **which** for animals and things and **where** for places.

*She's the woman **who** manages the restaurant.*
*I work for a company **which** makes toys.*
*Is this the city **where** Uncle Jim works?*

## 7 Circle the correct words.

1 Is she the woman **who** / **where** teaches at your school?
2 That's the detective **which** / **who** lives next door to me.
3 Is this the job **who** / **which** you asked about?
4 That's the office **which** / **where** I used to work.
5 Is this the desk **which** / **who** you use?

## 8 Complete the sentences with who, which or where.

1 The chef ______________ works at lunchtime isn't very good.
2 He knows ______________ your tools are.
3 Is that the dog ______________ works with the police?
4 Is this a career ______________ interests you?
5 Most of the people ______________ work here are women.

## 9 Listen to Carla and her mum and tick the correct picture. TR: 12.8

1 Where does Carla's mum work?

2 Who is the new employee?

3 Which day did the other employee start?

4 Who is going to talk to the new employee?

### SOUNDS OF ENGLISH TR: 12.9

A Read these pairs of words aloud.

| | | | | |
|---|---|---|---|---|
| 1 | lit | ☐ | lid | ☐ |
| 2 | mat | ☐ | mad | ☐ |
| 3 | food | ☐ | foot | ☐ |
| 4 | could | ☐ | cut | ☐ |
| 5 | bad | ☐ | but | ☐ |

B Now listen and tick the words you hear.

# Lesson 3

**1** **Listen and read each person's goals. Whose plan sounds best to you?** TR: 12.10

## What do you want to be?

**Jian** I'm not sure what I'm going to do. I used to think about getting a job as a police officer or a detective, but I don't think I'm brave enough. I enjoy playing football, but I'm not good enough to be a professional. So, I want two part-time jobs. I'd like to be a football coach. I also want to be an artist because I love painting. This would let me turn my hobbies into jobs!

**Tori** I know exactly what I'm going to do. I have always loved cooking so I'm going to be a chef. I'll go to college for about two years where I'll learn all about cooking. Then I'll work in a kitchen until I can become a real chef. I'm going to buy a restaurant and have lots of staff to help me! If I'm lucky, I will even have a TV show.

**Eliza** I love animals more than anything. I've wanted to be a vet since I was ten. You have to study for about seven years, and you have to be very clever and get good marks for all your exams. You must have work experience with animals, too. My only worry is that seeing so many sick animals will make me sad.

**2** **Circle the letter for the correct answer.**

1 Jian isn't good enough to be a _____.
 **a** professional football player **b** a detective

2 Jian wants _____.
 **a** to be a police officer **b** two part-time jobs

3 Tori _____ what she wants to be.
 **a** knows **b** doesn't know

4 Tori wants to buy _____.
 **a** a TV **b** a restaurant

5 Eliza will study for _____ years.
 **a** two **b** seven

6 Eliza thinks being a vet might make her _____.
 **a** sad **b** lazy

### SAY IT LIKE THIS!

**Talking about jobs**

What do you want to be when you grow up?
I want to be a … because …
*I want to be a chef because I'm good at cooking.*
I'm (very) good at/I enjoy …, so I want to be a …
*I enjoy helping people, so I want to be a doctor.*
You need qualifications/experience/skills.
*Mechanics need certain skills.*

**Talk to your partner about what you want to be. Use some of these phrases and practise the language above.**

working indoors/outdoors
fixing machines/cars
explaining things
helping people

**3 Listen to the conversation and circle the correct words.** TR: 12.11

1 Maria wants to be a **doctor** / **teacher**.

2 Doctors need good **staff** / **experience**.

3 Kevin's **dad** / **cousin** is a doctor.

4 Kevin doesn't want to be a **taxi driver** / **pilot** now.

5 Peter **enjoys** / **doesn't enjoy** his job.

6 Maria's sister is a **chef** / **manager**.

**4 Look at the pictures. Explain what these people are good at and say what is good and bad about their jobs.**

manager

mechanic

reporter

vet

## WRITING Making notes

**A We can make notes to help us write something. We write the notes next to headings for each paragraph.**

**B Look at the notes below. Put the notes under the correct headings.**

- no travel
- long hours
- you decide what you do
- paid a lot of money
- you make beautiful things
- sometimes hard to make money
- dangerous

| Worst job: | *pilot* |
|---|---|
| Why is it bad? | |
| One good thing | |
| Favourite job: | *artist* |
| Why is it good? | |
| One bad thing | |

**C Read the article from a school magazine. Underline the information from the notes in Part B. Which paragraphs do they appear in?**

### The best and the worst jobs

There are many different jobs, and it may be hard to decide. Everybody likes to do different things for different reasons.

My favourite job is that of an artist. You can make beautiful things and you don't have to travel to get to work. Also, you don't have to do what other people tell you.

You can decide what you are going to create and then you just do it. The only bad thing is that it's sometimes hard to make money as an artist.

The worst job I can think of is a pilot. You have to work for long hours and it's really tiring. If you make a mistake, things can go seriously wrong. That makes it too dangerous. The only good thing is that pilots are paid a lot of money, but money isn't the most important thing about a job.

In conclusion, every job has both good and bad things about it, but I think that artists have got the best jobs.

**D Write notes about the best and the worst jobs you can think of, and then write an article for your school magazine. Use this plan to help you.**

**Paragraph 1: Introduction**
Write two sentences to introduce the topic.

**Paragraph 2: The best job**
Explain why this is the best job. Say if there is anything bad about it.

**Paragraph 3: The worst job**
Explain why this is the worst job. Say if there is anything good about it.

**Paragraph 4: Conclusion**
Write one sentence to conclude your article.

**E Remember to check that you have included all your notes in your article.**

# Review

## 1 Label the photos.

______

______

______

______

______

______

## 2 Complete the table.

chef bike lane escalator manager
mechanic motorbike reporter tram

|  Transport |  Jobs |
|---|---|
| ______ | ______ |
| ______ | ______ |
| ______ | ______ |
| ______ | ______ |

## 3 Circle the correct answers.

1 A(n) **inspector** / **detective** got on the bus and we had to show her our tickets.

2 The policeman isn't wearing his uniform today because it's his **day off** / **destination**.

3 At the beginning of your **career** / **display**, you won't earn a lot of money.

4 Have you got any **employee** / **experience** as a chef?

5 Hurry up and **get on** / **check** the bus before the doors close.

## 4 Complete the sentences with the correct comparative or superlative structure and the adjectives in brackets.

1 This is ______ (good) train journey we've ever been on!

2 I think my mum's new job is ______ (bad) her old one.

3 I think a taxi for four people is ______ (cheap) as the tram.

4 We stayed in ______ (expensive) hotel in Hong Kong! It was beautiful!

5 This boat trip on the river was much ______ (interesting) the museum.

6 The bus is much ______ (slow) the Metro.

7 What's ______ (exciting) holiday you've ever had?

8 Your bike is as ______ (big) mine.

## 5 Complete the sentences with these words.

both either enough neither too

1 In this company, you can work ______ full-time or part-time.

2 You work ______ hard. Why don't you take a day off?

3 You can be ______ a doctor nor a vet with these marks!

4 We don't have ______ money for the plane. Let's go by train.

5 Do we have to choose just one country? Why can't we visit ______ of them?

**6** **Complete the sentences with adverbs formed from the adjectives in brackets.**

1 The manager talked ____________ (slow) while the employees took notes.

2 They left work ____________ (happy) because our manager let them go early.

3 The baby was washed ____________ (careful) by the nurse.

4 The message came ____________ (noisy) over the loudspeaker.

5 Reporters work in the field and in the studio. They usually work very ____________ (hard).

6 If you do ____________ (good) in your exams, you will get a good job.

**7** **Choose the correct answers.**

1 Is he the doctor ____ looks after your grandmother?

**a** where **b** who **c** which

2 My brother and his wife drive an electric car ____ they bought last year.

**a** where **b** which **c** who

3 Is that the restaurant ____ your mother is a chef?

**a** where **b** which **c** who

4 That's the artist ____ painted those pictures.

**a** where **b** which **c** who

5 Let's get the bus ____ goes to the airport.

**a** where **b** which **c** who

6 Is Mrs Cole the manager ____ you're going to work for?

**a** where **b** which **c** who

**8** **Compare two jobs or means of transport. Use comparatives, as well as both or neither in your answer.**

## Song

TR: 12.12

There are bikes, cars, buses and trams
in town.
Taxis, too! The metro's under the ground.
We can sail on a ferry, we can get on
a plane
Or travel through Europe on a new,
fast train.
The best thing is, we can go anywhere
By train, road, sea or up in the air.

Travelling takes us to different places
Visiting countries, seeing different faces.
Transport takes us where we want to go,
Around the world or just back home.

Flying's more expensive than going by car,
But it's the fastest way to go if you're
travelling far.
Riding a bike is good for everyone.
It's faster than walking and it's a lot
of fun.

# Video

**1** BEFORE YOU WATCH

**Who do you think has the best job? Circle.**

a detective
a chef
a sailor
an artist
a mechanic
a photographer
an author
a designer
a manager

____________________ has the best job.

**Now talk about why it's the best job.**

Sailors have the best job because they work on a yacht and travel a lot.

No way! A photographer has the best job and has to travel, too!

**2** WORDS TO KNOW

**Match the words to the pictures.**

submarine swordfish sea cucumber

____________

____________

____________

## 3 WHILE YOU WATCH

**Answer the questions while you watch the video.**

1 How many people are in the submarine? __________

2 How many turtles do the scientists see? __________

3 On their trip, the scientists see a swordfish. Is it swimming fast, slowly or both? __________

4 Do the scientists reach the sea floor? __________

## 4 AFTER YOU WATCH

**Tick T for *True* or F for *False*.**

1 The submarine crew sees a swordfish. T F

2 The underwater animals are attracted to the submarine's lights. T F

3 There are men and women in the submarine. T F

4 Jessica Cramp works to save sharks and other fish. T F

## 5 WATCH AGAIN

**Now talk about going in a submarine. Describe your trip and what you saw.**

I saw sharks and whales. It was the best trip ever!

The submarine travelled slowly to the bottom of the sea. I saw the most beautiful fish everywhere!

# Grammar Reference

## Unit 1

### GRAMMAR Present simple

We use the present simple to talk about:

**a** general truths.
*It **rains** a lot in winter here.*

**b** things we do regularly.
*I **visit** my uncle every summer.*

**c** permanent states.
*Uncle Omar **lives** on a farm.*

### GRAMMAR Adverbs of frequency

We use these adverbs to show how often we do something.
*My friends **sometimes** come to my house.*

**always → usually → often → sometimes → never**
100% of the time ←――――――→ 0% of the time

Adverbs of frequency go before the main verb:
*They **never see** Grandad.*

**But** they go **after** the verb **be**:
*My friend **is never** on time.*

Except in a question:
***Is** your mum **always** so nice?*

You can ask questions with **How often**.
***How often** do you go on holiday?*

### GRAMMAR Present continuous

We use the present continuous to talk about:

**a** things that are temporary or are happening now or around now.
*Uncle Dan **is eating** breakfast.*
*He**'s not having** tea with his breakfast.*

**b** fixed future plans.
*I**'m visiting** my friend tomorrow.*
***Are** you **coming** with us?*

**c** what is happening in a picture.
*In this picture, the lion cub **is playing**.*
***Is** its mother **sleeping** in the picture?*
*No, she **isn't**.*

**Time expressions** now, at the moment, today, this morning, tomorrow

### GRAMMAR Present simple and present continuous

We use the present simple to talk about general truths, things we do regularly and permanent states.
*We **live** in a big house.*

We use the present continuous to talk about things that are temporary or are happening now or around now, for fixed future plans and to say what is happening in a picture.
*I**'m going out** with my cousin tomorrow.*

**Note:** There are some verbs that we don't use with continuous tenses. These are called **stative verbs** and they include *know, like, love, think, understand* and *want*.

## Unit 2

### GRAMMAR Past simple (regular verbs)

We use the past simple for:

**a** things that started and finished in the past.
*We **moved** here last year.*
***Did** you **live** nearby?*
*No, we **didn't**.*

**b** things that happened one after the other in the past.
*We **cleaned** the house, **opened** the door and **walked** down the street.*

**c** habits in the past.
*I **tidied** my bedroom every Friday night.*

**Time expressions**

yesterday
last night/week/month/year
two days/a month/a year ago
in October/2007

### GRAMMAR Past simple (irregular verbs)

We do not add **-ed** for the past simple affirmative of irregular verbs.

*Mum **gave** my aunt a vacuum cleaner.*

*We **got** a new bookcase yesterday.*

## Unit 3

### GRAMMAR Past continuous

We use the past continuous to:

**a** talk about things that were happening at a particular time in the past.
*Last night we **were painting** pictures.*

**b** talk about two or more things that were happening at the same time in the past.
*At eight o'clock, my little sister **was drawing** and I **was reading** a book.*

**c** to set the scene of a story.
*It **was snowing** and we **were making** a snowman.*

**Time expressions**

all day yesterday
all morning
at 3 o'clock
last Thursday
last year
this morning
at this time last week/year
from three o'clock till four

**Affirmative**

I/he/she/it was walking
you/we/they were walking

**Negative**

I/he/she/it wasn't (was not) walking
you/we/they weren't (were not) walking

**Questions**

Was I/he/she/it walking?
Were you/we/they walking?

**Short answers**

Yes, I/he/she/it was.
Yes, we/you/they were.
No, I/he/she/it wasn't.
No, we/you/they weren't.

### GRAMMAR Past simple and past continuous

We can use the past simple and the past continuous in the same sentence to:

**a** show one past action interrupted another one.
*I **was watching** a film when I **heard** the doorbell.*

**b** tell a story in the past.
*The divers **were taking** photos underwater when a shark **swam** by.*

We usually use *when* and *while* to connect the two actions. We use *when* before the past simple and *while* before the past continuous.

*We were playing football **when** it **started** to rain.*
*I had a brilliant idea **while** I **was watching** television.*

### GRAMMAR Used to

We use **used to** to talk about:

**a** actions that happened often in the past but don't happen now.
*We **used to go** to the gym every day.*

**b** states that existed in the past but don't exist now.
*I **used to love** skiing but now I think it's boring.*

When we use a negative, we say **didn't use to**.
*Dad **didn't use to** cook very often.*

We use a bare infinitive after **used to**.

**Affirmative**

I/he/she/it/you/we/they used to play

**Negative**

I/he/she/it/you/we/they didn't use to play

**Question**

Did I/he/she/it/you/we/they use to play … ?

**Short answers**

Yes, I/he/she it/we/you/they did.
No, I/he/she it/we/you/they didn't.

# Grammar Reference

## Unit 4

### GRAMMAR Much, many

We use **much** and **many** to describe quantities. We use **much** in negative sentences and questions with uncountable nouns and we use **many** in affirmative and negative sentences and questions with plural countable nouns.

*Guy hasn't got **much** lemonade.*

*There aren't **many** apples in the bowl.*

We use **How much/many** … **?** to ask about quantities of countable and uncountable things.

***How much** money have you got**?***

***How many** bananas did you eat**?***

### GRAMMAR A lot of, lots of, a few, a little

We use **a lot of** or **lots of** with countable and uncountable nouns in affirmative and negative sentences and questions.

*There are **a lot of** bananas on that tree.*

*There is **lots of** water in the jug.*

We use **a few** with countable nouns in affirmative sentences and questions.

*Robbie ate **a few** crisps.*

We use **a little** with uncountable nouns in affirmative sentences and questions.

*Is there **a little** milk in the fridge?*

### GRAMMAR Some, any, every, no

We use **some** and **any** when it isn't important how many people, things or places there are. We use **some** for affirmative sentences and **any** for negative sentences and questions.

*I want **some** cakes, please.*

*There aren't **any** people at the table.*

We use **every** when we talk about all people, things or places. It has a positive meaning and we use it with a singular verb form.

***Every** restaurant in town is expensive.*

We use **no** when we talk about no person, thing or place. **No** has a negative meaning but we use it with an affirmative verb form.

*There were **no** sauces on the table.*

### GRAMMAR Indefinite pronouns

We use **somebody**, **something** and **somewhere** to talk about one person, thing or place in affirmative sentences.

***Somebody** ate my dinner.*

We use **anybody**, **anything** and **anywhere** to talk about one person, thing or place in negative sentences and questions.

*Is there **anything** for lunch? I'm really hungry.*

We use **everybody**, **everything** and **everywhere** to talk about all people, things or places but we use them with a singular verb form.

*I looked **everywhere**, but I didn't find the eggs.*

We use **nobody**, **nothing** and **nowhere** to talk about no person, thing or place. We use an affirmative verb with these words but the meaning of the sentence is negative.

*We're hungry because we had **nothing** for lunch.*

## Unit 5

### GRAMMAR Present perfect simple

We use the present perfect simple to say what:

**a** started in the past and is still happening.
*Sally's not at school. She**'s gone** to the dentist.*

**b** has just finished.
*I**'ve just finished** my homework. Now, let's play!*

**c** happened in the past without saying when.
*The head teacher **has been** very busy this week.*

**d** happened in the past but affects the present.
*He**'s broken** his hand so he can't write.*

To form this tense, use *have* and the past participle of the main verb.

### GRAMMAR For, since, already, just, never

We use **for** to show a period of time and **since** to show when something started.

*I **have been** at this school **for** six months.*

*They **have been** in class 5B **since** the autumn.*

We use **already** to show a time before now and **just** to talk about a recent event.

*We**'ve already had** a maths test this week.*

*I**'ve just had** a brilliant idea.*

We use **never** to talk about things that haven't happened so far. We use an affirmative verb with **never** but the meaning is negative.

*I**'ve never had** a C in geography.*

### GRAMMAR Present perfect simple

**Negative**

I haven't (have not) eaten.
He/She/It hasn't (he/she/it has not) eaten.
We/You/They haven't (have not) eaten.

**Questions**

Have I eaten?
Has he/she/it eaten?
Have we/you/they eaten?

**Short answers**

Yes, I have. / No, I haven't.
Yes, he/she/it has. / No, he/she/it hasn't.
Yes, we/you/they have.
No, we/you/they haven't.

### GRAMMAR Ever, yet

We use **ever** in questions to ask about things that have happened up to now. **Ever** comes before the past participle in the sentence.

*Have you **ever** been away on a school trip?*

We use **yet** with negatives and questions when we want to say *until now*. **Yet** comes at the end of the sentence.

*Have you cleaned the board **yet**?*

*I haven't studied for my exam **yet**.*

### GRAMMAR Present perfect simple and *How long*

We can use **How long** with the present perfect simple to ask questions about the length of time something has happened.

***'How long have** you **lived** here?' 'Three years.'*

***'How long have** you **taught** French?' 'Two months.'*

# Grammar Reference

## Unit 6

### GRAMMAR Past simple and present perfect simple

We use the past simple for:

**a** things that started and finished in the past.
*I **hurt** my elbow last night.*

**b** things that happened one after the other.
*I **opened** the door, **fell** on the floor and **hit** my head.*

**c** habits in the past.
*When I was a child, I **wore** socks in bed.*

**Time expressions for past simple:**
yesterday, last night/week/month/year, three days/a month/a year ago, in January/2014

We use the present perfect simple to talk about things that:

**a** started in the past and are still happening.
*My leg **has hurt** for three days.*

**b** have just finished.
*I**'ve just washed** my hands.*

**c** happened in the past but we don't say exactly when.
*He **has fallen off** the horse twice.*

**d** happened in the past but have a result which affects the present.
*I**'ve walked** all around the park, and now I'm tired.*

**Time expressions for present perfect simple:**
ever, never, already, just, for, since, yet

### GRAMMAR Possessive pronouns

We use possessive pronouns when something belongs to someone or when someone has a particular relationship with something.

*That necklace is **mine**!*

A possessive pronoun replaces a possessive adjective and a noun.

*That's her medicine. = It's **hers**.*

We can also use possessive pronouns with *so* to agree with someone.

*'My hands are cold.' 'So are **hers**.'*
*'My head hurts.' 'So does **mine**.'*

**Possessive adjectives**
my his her your our their

**Possessive pronouns**
mine his hers yours ours theirs

## Unit 7

### GRAMMAR Future simple

We use the future simple:

**a** for predictions about the future.
*It **will rain** all day tomorrow.*

**b** for decisions that we make now.
*I**'ll look after** the plants.*

**c** for offers, promises and warnings.
*Don't touch that dog, it **will bite** you.*

**d** to ask someone for help.
***Will** you **feed** the birds, please?*

**e** after **think** and **be sure**:
*I**'m sure** the soil **will be** wet.*

### GRAMMAR Be going to

We use **be going to**:

**a** to talk about future plans and intentions.
*I**'m going to be** in Costa Rica in June.*

**b** to predict that something will happen when we have some proof or information.
*It**'s going to rain** later. They said so on TV.*

### GRAMMAR Gerunds

Gerunds are nouns which we make from verbs. We add **–ing** to the verb to form them. We can use gerunds:

**a** as the subject of a sentence.
***Playing** with snakes can be dangerous.*

**b** as the object of a sentence.
*I like **running** in the fields.*

**c** after prepositions.
*I'm not very good at **looking** after plants.*

**d** after verbs such as **can't stand**, **dislike**, **like**, **love**, **enjoy**, **miss**, **hate** and **remember**.
*I **enjoy feeding** the squirrels.*

### GRAMMAR Question tags

We use question tags:

**a** to confirm our opinion.
*This forest is amazing, **isn't it**?*

**b** when we are pretty sure that what we say is true.
*You've got a big garden, **haven't you**?*

We make question tags with an auxiliary verb and a subject pronoun. We use the auxiliary verb that we use for the tense in the main part of the sentence.

*Those dogs aren't running, **are they**?*

For affirmative sentences in the present simple we use **do**/**does** and for sentences in the past simple we use **did**.

*They didn't go to see the turtles, **did they**?*

When the sentence uses a verb in the affirmative, we use a negative question tag. When the sentence uses a verb in the negative, we use an affirmative question tag.

*We go to the park often, **don't we**?*

*He hasn't been to Bora Bora this year, **has he**?*

We can use questions tags in all tenses and with modal verbs.

*Elephants can swim, **can't they**?*

# Grammar Reference

## Unit 8

### GRAMMAR First conditional

We use the first conditional to talk about something which will probably happen in the present or in the future. Sentences in the first conditional have two clauses. The *if* clause uses *if* followed by the present simple, and the result clause uses the future simple.

***If we recycle** batteries, **we will help** the environment.*

In the first conditional, one or both of the clauses can be negative.

*If you **don't recycle**, we **will have** a lot of rubbish!*

*If we **don't look after** our beaches, they **won't be** clean.*

We can ask questions with first conditional sentences with and without question words:

*What will happen if we destroy the environment?*

*Will this rubbish smell bad if we leave it here?*

**Note:** It doesn't matter which clause comes first, but if we put the *if* clause first then we use a comma. If the result clause comes first, we don't use a comma.

*If you grow flowers, your garden will be beautiful.*

*Your garden will be beautiful if you grow flowers.*

### GRAMMAR Second conditional

We use the second conditional:

**a** to talk about something that cannot happen in the present or the future.
*If I had** a garden, **I'd be** very happy!*

**b** to talk about something that is unlikely to happen in the present or the future.
*That plant **would die if** you **watered** it twice a day.*

**c** to give advice.
***If** I **were** you, I**'d start** recycling.*

Sentences in the second conditional have two clauses. The *if* clause uses *if* followed by the past simple and the result clause uses **would** followed by a bare infinitive.
*I **wouldn't destroy** that **if** I **were** you.*

In the second conditional, one or both of the clauses can be negative.
*The city **would be** very dirty if we **didn't recycle**.*
*If we **didn't keep** our beaches clean, they **wouldn't be** nice.*

We can ask questions with second conditional sentences with and without question words:

*What would happen to the animals if there was a fire in the forest?*

*Would they throw away plastic bottles if they didn't see a bin?*

**Note:** We usually use **were** instead of **was** after the first and third person singular.

## Unit 9

### GRAMMAR Have to

We can use **have to** to talk about obligation in the present, the future and the past.
We use a bare infinitive after **have to**.

*You will **have to** go to the city centre.*

*Yesterday we **had to** walk home because we missed the bus.*

### GRAMMAR Must

We use **must** to talk about obligation in the present and the future. We use a bare infinitive after **must**.

*You **must** buy a ticket for the bus.*

*We **mustn't** be late tomorrow.*

***Must** you make so much noise? Yes, I **must**.*

**Note:** We use **don't have to** to show that something isn't necessary but we can choose to do it if we want.

*You **don't have to** buy books – there's a library in town.*
We use **mustn't** when we want to say we are not allowed to do something.
*You **mustn't** throw rubbish in the street.*

### GRAMMAR Can and could

We use **can** for the present and the future to:

**a** talk about ability.
*We **can** climb walls.*

**b** ask for and give permission.
***Can** I touch the statue, please?*
*You **can't** eat or drink in the museum.*

**c** talk about what is possible.
*You **can** walk around the park all day.*

We use **could** to talk about ability and possibility in the past.

*He **could** walk when he was one year old.*

*We **couldn't** see the theatre from the park.*

We use a bare infinitive after **can** and **could**.

### GRAMMAR Might

We use **might** to talk about possibility.
*It **might** rain tomorrow.*
We use a bare infinitive after **might**.
*If you don't like noise, you **might not** have fun in the city.*

### GRAMMAR Should

We use **should** to ask for and give advice.

*You **should** be careful in the city at night.*

***Should** I turn right at Bank Street?*
We use a bare infinitive after **should**.
*They **shouldn't** talk so much during the film.*

## Unit 10

### GRAMMAR Present simple passive

We use the passive voice:

**a** when we are more interested in the action than the person doing it.
*A lot of televisions **are made** in China.*

**b** when we don't know who does the action.
*The news **is shown** every hour.*

**c** when it is obvious who does the action.
*Television **is watched** in a lot of countries.*

If we want to talk about the person doing the action, we use **by**:
*The news **isn't read by** a local reporter.*
We make the present simple passive with **am**, **are** or **is** and the past participle of the main verb.

### GRAMMAR Past simple passive

We make the past simple passive with **was** or **were** and the past participle of the main verb.

# Grammar Reference

## Unit 11

### GRAMMAR Comparatives and superlatives

We use the comparative form to compare two or more people, animals or things. We often use the word **than** after the comparative form.

We add **-er** to short adjectives.

*A bus is **faster than** a bicycle.*

We don't add **-er** to long adjectives, but we use the word **more** before the adjective.

*Travelling by train is **more interesting than** travelling by boat.*

We can use (**not**) **as** + adjective + **as** to compare two things.

*The bus is **as cheap as** the tram.*

*This seat **isn't as comfortable as** that one.*

We use the superlative form to compare a person, an animal or thing with many other people, animals or things. We add **-est** to short adjectives and use the word **the** before the adjective.

*These tickets are **the cheapest**.*

We don't add **-est** to long adjectives, but we use the word **most** before the adjective.

*These tickets are **the most expensive**.*

Look at these irregular forms:

| Adjective | Comparative | Superlative |
|---|---|---|
| good | **better** | **the best** |
| bad | **worse** | **the worst** |

### GRAMMAR Too and enough

We use **too** to show that there is more of something than we need and that this is a problem. It is followed by an adjective.

*The bus is **too slow**, so let's get the metro.*

We use **enough** to show that there is as much of something as we need. It comes after an adjective.

*I've washed the car.*
*Is it **clean enough** now?*

We can also use **enough** before uncountable nouns and plural countable nouns to show that there is less of something than we need and that this is a problem.

*I didn't have **enough money** for a taxi.*

*Did we buy **enough tickets** for everyone?*

### GRAMMAR Both, either, neither

We use **both**, **either** and **neither** to talk about two people, animals or things.

We use **both** with affirmative verbs. It means *one and the other.*

*I have travelled by **both** train **and** bus.*

***Both** cities have got good railways.*

We use **either** with affirmative and negative verbs. It means *one or the other*. It is followed by **or** or **of**.

*You can use **either** a ticket **or** a travel card.*

*I can't use **either of** these means of transport.*

We use **neither** with affirmative verbs, but it has got a negative meaning. It means not one and not the other. It is followed by **nor** or **of**.

***Neither** a taxi **nor** a car is a good choice.*

***Neither of** the trams was on time.*

## Unit 12

### GRAMMAR Adverbs of manner

We use adverbs of manner to describe how we do something. We make most adverbs by adding **-ly** to the adjective, but if the adjective ends in **-y**, we take off the **-y** and add **-ily**:

| Adjective | Adverb |
|---|---|
| quick | quick**ly** |
| lazy | laz**ily** |

*The artist paints **beautifully**.*

*The detective caught the thief **easily**.*

Some adverbs are irregular:

| Adjective | Adverb |
|---|---|
| hard | hard |
| fast | fast |
| high | high |
| right | right |
| wrong | wrong |
| good | well |

### GRAMMAR Relative clauses

We use relative clauses to give more information about people, animals and things. A relative clause begins with a relative pronoun or adverb. We use **who** for people, **which** for animals and things and **where** for places.

*She's the woman **who** manages the restaurant.*

*I work for a company **which** makes toys.*

*Is this the city **where** Uncle Jim works?*

***Wonderful World 4*, Second Edition**

Vice President, Editorial Director:
John McHugh

Executive Editor: Siân Mavor

Commissioning Editor: Kayleigh Buller

Senior Development Editor:
Karen Haller Beer

Media Research: Leila Hishmeh

Head of Strategic Marketing EMEA ELT:
Charlotte Ellis

Product Marketing Executive:
Ellen Setterfield

Head of Production: Celia Jones

Content Project Manager:
Sue Povey / Jonathan Beck

Manufacturing Manager: Eyvett Davis

Art Director: Brenda Carmichael

Cover Design: Lisa Trager

Interior Design and Composition: Symmetry

Audio Producer: James Richardson



Student Edition: Level 4
ISBN: 978-1-473-76046-2

**National Geographic Learning**
Cheriton House, North Way, Andover, Hampshire, SP10 5BE, United Kingdom



Printed in Greece by Bakis SA
Print number: 01 Print Year: 2018